I0035220

Maximize Your Health Insurance

Strategies to Keep More Money in Your Pocket

William J. Pokluda, CEBS

Copyright © 2017

by William J. Pokluda, CEBS

All Right Reserved

March 2025

Cover Design:

Elisa N. Santiago

ISBN – 13: 978-0998823805 ISBN-
10: 0998823805

www.maximizehealthinsurance.com

Are You Getting the Most from Your Health Insurance Plan?

Don't leave money on the insurance table

Understand your health insurance now so you can benefit from it <u>later</u> when you really need it

Contents

Introduction

When it comes to health insurance, people are leaving money on the table. Why does this happen?

According to the Employee Benefit Research Institute, 68% of people spend an hour or less researching benefit options during the annual open enrollment period.[1] An Aflac study reported how only 51% had an understanding of what their total annual cost would be, and only 39% of employees felt they had a full understanding of their health insurance policy.[2]

With the cost of health insurance so high for many, and with many of us responsible for sharing in the cost of health care delivery through higher deductibles and coinsurance, why wouldn't we spend more time making sure we understand what our options are and identify ways to increase the value of the benefit choices we have, putting more money into our pocket?

There are a number of reasons people give for not spending sufficient time thinking about their health insurance:

- "It takes too much time which I don't have."
- "It's not important, or not a priority."
- "I'm relatively healthy, so I'm not going to worry."
- "It was too confusing, so I gave up."
- "I picked the plan that my parent, friend, or colleague enrolled in."
- "We kept the same plan we've had for years. It's just easier."
- "I just took the default plan my company enrolled me in."

I'm sure you can think of a few more reasons of your own. Of those who do take the time and change benefits, they typically spend about two hours each year studying their options. As a result of the extra time and effort spent studying their options, they changed their benefit options for a number of valid and pertinent reasons:

- New plans were offered by the employer
- A better plan was available than what they were currently enrolled in
- There was an increase in the cost of benefits

Even if we take the time to evaluate our benefit options and make a rational decision, often that's the last time we think about our health insurance. Our insurance comes into play again only when we really need it, like when we're sick or have an unexpected illness, are in an accident that results in medical bills, or we reluctantly need to get an annual checkup or blood test.

Our interest in insurance is peaked when we start getting bills in the mail from the health care provider. Sticker shock hits us after opening the envelope. We start to read the billing invoice, but our eyes glaze over it as we're overwhelmed or confused. What does it all mean?

Often, I hear people say, "I have insurance, why do I owe so much?" It's after the dust settles that we open our eyes to what's going on and we may have missed a few good opportunities to save money or prevent such high sticker shock.

What's really at stake?

It's estimated that in 2023 92% of the U.S. population were enrolled in some type of health plan. Of those with a health plan, 53.7% are enrolled through their employer at some point in the calendar year, followed by Medicaid (18.9%), Medicare (18.9%), direct-purchase (10.2%), TRICARE (2.6%), and VA (1.0%) leaving 8.0% of the population uninsured.[3.] The percentage enrollment doesn't add up to 100% because of overlap in enrollment across different plans.

The average annual premium for single coverage was $8,951 and $ 25,572 for family coverage. 81% of employers cover up to 25% of the single coverage premium, and 58% of employers cover up to 25% of the family coverage premium. Employees are left paying a large portion of the remaining health plan premium. Beyond that, people still have to pay out-of-pocket costs towards annual deductibles which averaged $1,787 in 2023 for a single person and typically twice that or more for family coverage. And then there's the coinsurance (20% - 30%) we owe after the deductible is met.[4]

In comparison, the annual premium cost of Healthcare.gov marketplace plans for single coverage can cost upward of $5,500 on average (before government subsidies kick in). The average Marketplace deductible in 2022 ranged between $4,890 for a Silver plan and $7,481 for a Bronze plan.[5]

Just how real is the struggle with medical expenses? Pretty real. According to Motley Fool Money, 45% of Americans can afford a $400 expense with funds from their checking or savings account, with only 54% able to cover three months of expenses with savings. A significant or catastrophic health situation could put someone at serious risk of being unable to pay for their expenses.[6]

Bottom line: Health insurance can cost us a lot of money directly and indirectly.

If you obtain your health insurance through your employer, you're most likely paying portion of the total premium cost through payroll deductions. The premium is what an insurance company requires be paid, usually on a monthly basis, for use of the insurance plan. Employers tend to subsidize the majority of premiums which is increasingly becoming a burden financially.

Employers are challenged with balancing their ability to provide quality and affordable benefit choices while also remaining competitive as a business in the marketplace. Employers are adopting a pass-it-long strategy with increased deductibles, coinsurance and other cost-effective plan design features.

Employees may not have control over decisions their employers or the government make, but they can take an engaged role in understanding the ins and outs of their health insurance to ensure they're getting the most value from their plans, and NOT leaving any money on the table. You don't have to be a rocket scientist, an actuary, underwriter or a financial analyst to take control of your health insurance.

Are people engaging in consumer behavior related to their health insurance?

Ever since High Deductible Health Plans arrived on the scene, a myriad of financial accounts, such as health savings accounts and health reimbursement accounts, were touted as solutions to help stem the increase in health care costs. If people felt like they were in control of the money being spent on their health care, then they would be motivated to change their behavior to make cost-effective and quality-related decisions on their treatment.

Results are in. The vast majority of people have not been engaged in consumer behavior as it relates to their health insurance and health care. While 49.7% of privately insured Americans are enrolled in a high deductible health plan[9], all Americans enrolled in a privately insurance health insurance could potentially benefit in the long run, both financially and health wise, from engagement in consumer behaviors.

What exactly are these consumer behaviors?
- Saving for future health care services
- Discussing costs with a provider
- Comparing prices
- Comparing quality
- Trying to negotiate a price

The March 2019 edition of Health Affairs published the results of a comprehensive study of Americans with High-Deductible Health Plans illustrating these opportunities to enhance consumer behaviors. As a benefits professional, I can attest at least anecdotally and empirically that there are significant opportunities to enhance consumer behaviors. Generally speaking, each of these five consumer behaviors are aspirational, at best, within our current health care system.[10]

According to Kaiser Foundation, only 30% of Americans enrolled in a HDHP have either a health reimbursement account (HRA) or health savings account (HSA) included. This means that another 10% of those enrolled in a HDHP do not have the luxury of an HRA or HSA. Having these types of savings vehicles allows for individuals and employers to make tax-advantaged contributions to help offset the out-of-pocket costs associated with the first-dollar responsibility a deductible requires each of us to pay.

Why are so few Americans engaged in health care consumer behaviors?

Health insurance literacy (HIL) among Americans is low. HIL is not taught in schools. Rather, we learn "on-the-job" to navigate health insurance coverage when we're forced to get treatment or deal with medical bills after-the-fact.

The Health Insurance Literacy Expert Roundtable defined HIL as "the degree to which individuals have the knowledge, ability, and confidence to find and evaluate information about health plans, select the best plan for their own (or their family's) financial and health circumstances, and use the plan once enrolled.

Demonstrated high levels of HIL requires the mastery of a number of fundamental skill sets:

- **Compare** several health plans and key features to choose right one for you
- **Search** for an In-Network doctor. Assess the adequacy and fit of the provider network for health

and financial circumstances.

- **Understand cost-sharing** for office visits, prescription drugs and other medical services across a broad category of services
- **Assess the quality** of plans in terms of measures that are important, such as processing claims or customer service.

- **Use health insurance statements (EOBs) to** identify what you owe
- Know where to go for **help**
- **Understand** your appeal rights

Health Insurance Literacy skill sets run on a continuum starting with basic skills and then building up the ladder. Basic skills start off as a foundation. As the amount and complexity of health care services increases, the level of engagement and complexity is required to manage successful outcomes of your health insurance.

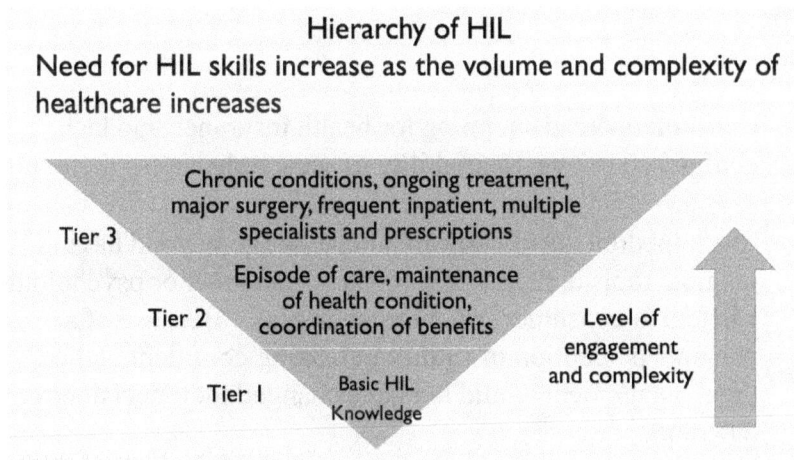

Hierarchy of HIL
Need for HIL skills increase as the volume and complexity of healthcare increases

Tier 3 Chronic conditions, ongoing treatment, major surgery, frequent inpatient, multiple specialists and prescriptions

Tier 2 Episode of care, maintenance of health condition, coordination of benefits

Level of engagement and complexity

Tier I Basic HIL Knowledge

Research literature is full of studies demonstrating how consumers struggle with cost-sharing and medical services terminology.

Consumers often stay in the same plan year after year, even when better choices are available. Adults cannot calculate an employee's share of health insurance costs. Then, one's ability to choose the "optimal" plan declines as the number of choices increase and the complexity of choices increases.

- 51% of Americans do not understand basic health insurance terms,[11]
- 84% of U.S. adults unable to calculate the employee's share of health insurance costs,[12]
- 62% of Americans don't always compare costs before receiving care,[13]
- Only 10% of Americans check whether a medical provider or facility is in-network when their health plan changes,[13]
- More than 77% of Americans misunderstand the concept of "coinsurance"[14]

Consumers dread shopping for health insurance and lack confidence in own their ability to accurately assess their choices.

The impediments of consumer behavior go beyond having tangible tools and practices in place. Personal or psychological barriers to consumer behavior are at play. Because of a person's perception of futility in making confident choice, their engagement would not have changed their decisions or outcomes.

Adverse Impact of Low Health Insurance Literacy
Researchers have speculated as to the adverse outcomes
associated with poor understanding of health insurance:

- Delays or failure to enroll in any health plan
- Reduced ability to access needed care effectively
- Delaying or avoiding care
- Correlation of poor health status with low HIL

Health outcomes would be higher if people knew how to find
a doctor, fill a prescription, know how to use and pay for that
medication, and understand their medical provider's
explanations.

What can be done to enhance consumer behavior?
Right now, emphasis is on the consumer to change their
behavior and take control. Unfortunately, until the healthcare
system changes, people need to do their homework, pay
attention and ask questions of their providers and health
insurance plans. ***Become health insurance literate.***
Employers and health plans can do more to promote, educate
and facilitate health insurance literacy. Health care providers
could develop practices to engage patients on the costs of
treatment options.

Financial impact of medical bills

Anyone can be impacted by medical bills. Medical bills are a
significant factor in bankruptcy filings. The Kaiser Family
Foundation showed that 41% of U.S. citizens carry some sort
of medical debt, and 24% were considering bankruptcy to
solve a medical debt issue.[7] Interestingly, another study
conducted by the Kaiser Family Foundation showed that the

majority of those who filed for bankruptcy due to medical expenses had some type of health insurance, thus debunking the myth that only the uninsured face financial catastrophes due to medical related expenses.[8]

While as many at 62% of bankruptcies include significant medical debt[7], a number of factors can contribute to someone filing for bankruptcy. The influence of medical bills alone on the cause of bankruptcy is probably hard to pinpoint as any number of factors can contribute:

- Lower income level
- Lost job
- Reduction of work hours resulting in loss of eligibility for insurance
- Taking time off of work to care for yourself or a family member with a health situation
- Unexpected or higher than normal medical expenses due to a catastrophic illness
- Additive effect of normal household and living expenses on top of increased medical bills

Among those with private health insurance who report having problems paying their medical bills, 46% have medical plans with high deductibles (at least $1,500 for an individual of $3,000 for a family). The other half with problems paying their medical bills have lower-deductible plans. [7]

Among those who report having a problem paying their medical bills, two-thirds (66%) say the bills were the result of a one-time or short- term medical expense such as a hospital stay or an accident, while 33% cite bills for treatment of chronic conditions that have built up over time.

Problems paying medical bills affects people regardless of whether they have health insurance or not. People having problems paying their medical bills also report having other types of debt: credit card, car loan, student loan, a mortgage or home loan, or debt owed to a payday lender.
Understanding how your health insurance works may not solve all of your financial problems, but it could help you manage the financial burden of health care costs.

What can you really do?

Be responsible, practical, and mindful.
There are numerous best practices one can take to stay in control of their health insurance. I will recommend a number of them in this book. You may also develop your own.

Be an active consumer of your health insurance.
When something goes awry with your health insurance, don't expect the insurance company or your benefits department or your doctor to call and fix it. You need to take an active part throughout the year. Many of us drop the bill from the doctor's office into our bills basket and prefer not to think about it because we don't know where to start, or it's too painful to delve into it.

Read the fine print.
This may be the hardest part, but can save you hundreds of dollars, or even more, just by paying attention. Ask lots of questions early and often of your health care provider, insurance company or employer. Don't make any assumptions.

Learn how to navigate the system.
Do you know how to access your health insurance account online? Do

you assume what the doctor says you owe is correct? Can you find a doctor In-Network? Does your plan require a referral or prior authorization to get covered? Are you aware of how to appeal a denied claim?

Keep a journal of your health insurance activity.
How do you keep track of your health insurance information? Do you have a file of your benefit plan documents, claims submitted and paid? While this seems like busy work or time wasted on shuffling papers around, your situation could quickly become a nightmare to manage if you don't already have a system of recording your health activity, such as claims submitted, insurance payments, inquiries made to doctors, insurance and collection agencies, names of insurance reps and their contact information. Become your very own insurance sleuth. It'll pay off in the end, even if it simply makes you feel better having control

Try to be healthy.
While the purpose of this book is to help you become an active consumer of your health insurance and ultimately help you get the most from your health insurance plan, there is an underlying theme about why we have so much health care consumption in the first place. True, there's been lots of scientific advancements and breakthroughs, but these often come at a cost which is typically borne by the average person through higher insurance rates. Yes, costs of health care advancement get passed on to employers and employees.

Pharmaceutical companies invest heavily in research and may only get a return on their investment on a handful or perhaps one special drug, which costs an arm and a leg. Therefore, the cost of drugs may be inflated to cover research costs, successes and failures.

At the end of the day, with the exception of genetic and environmental causes, our health is determined by our behavior: do we eat right? Do we exercise? Do we avoid unhealthy risks such as smoking? Some research estimates that 60% of chronic diseases can be prevented or at least minimized, and chronic diseases are estimated to cause the lion share of health care costs.

Are you asking the right questions about your health insurance?

It's true. Most of us don't make the time to review health insurance until we need it or it's too late. By the time we do need it, we realize we owe more money because we didn't make the right choices up front or are now incurring late fees or paying interest on medical debt. Picking the wrong medical plan may result in paying more out of pocket or not getting the right type of medical coverage we need.

In my professional experience, I often see people mistakes with their insurance benefits options or fail to take advantage of plan features readily available to them. The amount of money they lose or leave on the table is significant.

One employee I'll call Ted was a 40-something sales professional with a spouse and a two-year-old child. Ted recently transferred to my company where his prior employer provided an HMO plan, one where you only had to pay $10 copays for most visits. That was it. His wife loved it as she didn't have to pay much out of pocket. In fact, he bragged about how his spouse's maternity claims were fully paid by the HMO.

As a new hire to the organization, Ted was evaluating the new medical plan options and noticed we didn't offer an HMO. He observed how we offered several options each having a deductible higher than the

15

next. *So, you're telling me that I'm responsible for paying a deductible before the insurance will even start paying? That's ludicrous.* Sure, on the surface it seemed like a bad plan to join. I asked him, *Ted, how much were you paying each paycheck to be in that HMO plan at your prior employer?* The contributions to be in the lowest cost plan at my company was only $1,200 annually.

The next day Ted called me back to convey how he used to pay three times that amount in payroll contributions annually and had done so for the past several years while at his prior employer.
Holy cow! His wife loved paying those low copays, but she never saw what was coming out of his paycheck. She also seemed to be a frequent flyer with the pediatrician's office; every time their child came down with a minor cough or ailment, they went straight to the doctor's office.

The point is, you need to look under the hood at your plans and do a realistic evaluation, and comparison if needed to determine your best option.

Yes, our health is important, but so is having financial savvy. For the extra time you have to spend keeping track and managing your health insurance, consider it a way to invest in or pay yourself.

Do you have a trusted resource on your side?

Not everyone has a trusted resource they can go to who can/will take care of your health insurance questions, issues, or challenges. If you get your insurance through an employer, you probably have access to someone in Human Resources or the Benefits Department to call for direction. Often the first response is "Did you call the insurance company to see what they say?"

The employer HR or benefits team are not typically the experts in all- things insurance, especially when it comes to why a claim wasn't paid as expected. The employer's benefits resource often rely upon their insurance contacts to research and get answers. Due to HIPAA or privacy laws, people other than you or your family are not allowed to see your medical claims and personal health information unless you give them permission, so there's a limit to how much an HR or benefits resource can really do on your behalf which is why they may prefer to direct you to the insurance company for help. This is yet another reason why you need to be your own advocate.

Most of us are not insurance experts

We assume our employer or insurance company has our interests at heart. Why play the odds and hope for the best?

Do you rely upon the insurance representative at the doctor's office for direction? Doctor's offices are often the ones filing claims, verifying eligibility and deciphering what the insurance company paid, then telling you what you owe. Do you just accept/trust what they say you owe?

The health care professional is also a business, and they typically have hundreds, if not thousands, of patients. Their self-interest is cash flow, as they need to cover overhead, pay employees, and make a living. Do any of the following examples suggest that the doctor's office has your best financial interest at heart?

- Did you ever sign a statement at the doctor's note saying something like—no matter what—you are responsible for paying the costs of the visit, even if the insurance doesn't pay?

- What about getting charged for an appointment you couldn't make?

- Or paying interest on an invoice you're late on?

- Or paying a surcharge on an office visit because it was after normal work hours.

- Have to pay for a procedure when you went in for a preventive checkup, normally covered at 100%?

- Receive an invoice from the doctor just days after your visit stating you owe money, and the statement says insurance estimate is $0.00? The bill hasn't even been processed by the insurance company yet, and you're being asked to pay the bill, even though you've gone In-Network.

Most of the time, the system works. I don't want to paint a picture that the whole system is broken, that medical professionals are greedy, and that insurance companies are inept. People need to take ownership and understand their role in the overall insurance process.

The system __doesn't__ work 100% of the time

The insurance system works because of a myriad of interconnected, interdependent, and often juxtaposed processes. The insurance industry relies heavily upon the use of technology which significantly aided in the advancement of efficiency. It's estimated that 97% of health claims are submitted, processed, and paid electronically with minimal or no human intervention.[15] To a certain extent, this advancement has most likely helped to keep insurance costs lower, but not by a lot. The administrative costs of the insurance equation can represent 10 - 15% of the total costs, possibly lower. A vast majority of insurance costs hinge upon the actual health costs incurred. People are sick or need medical treatment which costs money to support.

Manual intervention in submitting and paying claims still plays a significant role in getting things done. No one person or no one system is perfect. Things will go wrong. It's not a matter of *if* they will, but rather *when* they will go wrong. Even though 97% of claims were submitted electronically (in 2022), the denial rate of claims across 1, 500 hospitals in the United States have increased from 9% in 2016 to 12% in 2022.[15]

Here's a list of common occurrences that can impact your wallet as a result of electronic or manual intervention in paying medical claims:

- The wrong medical procedure code is submitted on a claim leading to a denied claim or one that is and either the claim is paid at an incorrect rate affecting your financial responsibility.

- An incorrect diagnosis code on a claim causes a denial or incorrect payment.

- You went for a preventive visit which should be paid at 100%, but the claim was submitted with a primary diagnosis code. Therefore, it gets applied to your deductible and covered using coinsurance (not paid at 100%), resulting in money due by you.

- Insurance companies often request additional information from a provider before paying a claim. You're only one of hundreds of patients, the doctor may not respond timely, or at all to the insurance company's inquiry.

- The insurance claims system isn't programmed correctly; your company's or plan's benefits design may have changed, but the update was delayed or overlooked. As a result, claims are not paid as expected.

- Insurance company outsources claims processing to a third party who gets paid by volume potentially impacting accuracy.

- Because of the medical condition or treatment type, the claim needs approval by the insurance company, or a third party outsourced to manage approvals. Radiology, chiropractic, physical therapy and mental health are typical medical services that can require further scrutiny before a claim is paid. You may have insurance coverage for the type of service, but if sufficient information is not provided on a timely basis, the insurance company won't pay the claim.

- You have a mental health claim, possibly for a long-term inpatient stay and the provider is out-of-network. The insurance companies may attempt to negotiate a lower payment to the provider, holding up the claim.

- Insurance companies can ask your doctor to verify the medical necessity for providing services.

Insurance companies provide service guarantees to employer groups. If the insurance company doesn't meet the service guarantees, employers may get refunds on premiums or service fees paid.

Insurance companies are measured on a number of metrics, but two of the more common ones related to claims payments are— ***paying claims timely and accurately***. The passing grade is typically less than 100% accuracy or timeliness. Often, it can be 95% or 98% which means 2% to 5% of the time insurance companies can get it wrong and not be held accountable. People are the ones who suffer. The system isn't perfect which is why they can't set a goal of 100% timely and accurate claims payments.

Have you ever been one of the 5%?

While some people may never have a medical claim in a given year, and others can have dozens of medical claims, it's difficult to know how many people are actually impacted by less than acceptable claims payments. But given how nearly 200 million people get their health insurance through their employer or a private plan, and how many claims are processed every day, it's inevitable that a lot of people will be adversely impacted.

Healthcare and Insurance Landscape

The healthcare system in the United States is generally considered a private system in that healthcare providers operate independently of the government offering services directly to patients. Doctors, hospitals and other healthcare providers can treat patients who make appointments or other such as through an emergency or urgent type visit. There are exceptions to this premise, but for the most part healthcare providers can treat just about anyone.

Medical & Healthcare Provider Types		
Doctors	Medical Groups	Outpatient clinics
Primary care	Specialists	Radiology
Urgent Care	Hospitals / Emergency Room	Pathology
Physical Therapy	Laboratories	Mental Health
Ambulance	Anesthesiology	Durable medical equipment
Home health care	Pharmacies	Long term care & rehabilitation

The financing of such healthcare visits is where the line between healthcare and health insurance may get blurry or requires a deeper understanding requiring your health insurance literacy skill set to kick-in. The healthcare system in the United States has evolved to a point where your access to healthcare treatment is contingent upon the type of insurance you may have.

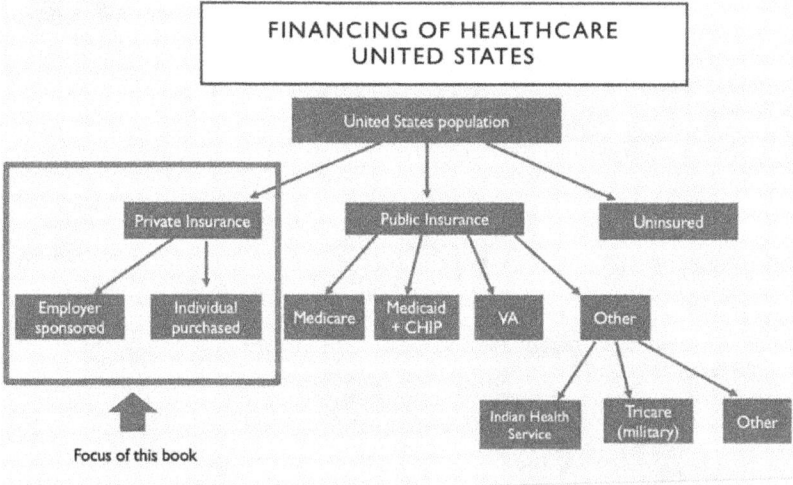

FINANCING OF HEALTHCARE
UNITED STATES

United States population

Private Insurance

Public Insurance

Uninsured

Employer sponsored

Individual purchased

Medicare

Medicaid + CHIP

VA

Other

Indian Health Service

Tricare (military)

Other

Focus of this book

One of the first questions a healthcare provider may ask you when scheduling an appointment is "what is your insurance?" Are you covered by a group/employer plan, Marketplace plan, Medicare, Medicaid, or are you a private payer without? The provider wants to know how they will be paid for your treatment.

Humana   Anthem. ✚🛡   United
                                     Healthcare

KAISER
PERMANENTE.   ꙮ Cigna.   MOLINA
                                    HEALTHCARE

♥aetna®   HCSC   Independence ✚
                 Health Care Service Corporation

There are a number of ways people in the United States obtain
health insurance. Throughout one's life, opportunities to be
insured become available based upon your need,
circumstance, job, or your stage in life. A majority of
Americans are covered through an employer plan, but with
the population aging, a larger number of people are enrolling
in Medicare. Beyond that, people obtain health insurance
through a variety of other ways:

- Private plans
- Individual market, including Marketplace plans (ACA)
- Employer groups
- Medicare (Medi-gap)
- Medicaid
- Veterans Administration
- College/School Plans
- Federal Government

Private insurance plans, including individual market, are offered locally in one's work or home state. Larger employers with employees based in multiple states offer regional or national-based plans, meaning you have health insurance coverage in a network nationally or in certain geographical regions.

Insurance Products (Alphabet soup)

Health insurance products have evolved over time to serve different needs and requirements. At the core of insurance is an essential philosophy that, in the event of a loss, the insurance plan will provide some type of benefit to replace that loss either in whole or in some other agreed upon manner. The insurance premiums paid to an insurance company are expected to cover the expected claims, plus cover administrative costs, and potentially have a little money left over to reinvest in the company or return as a profit if such company is a publicly traded firm.

Health insurance plans change due to competitive efforts to create new products and services, targeting population groups of different sizes, with different needs, and census make-up. These products have become a staple of our insurance jargon known by their acronyms.

HMO - Health Maintenance Organization
Typically limits coverage to care from doctors who work for or
contract with the HMO. It generally won't cover out-of-network
care except in an emergency. May require you to live or work
in its service area to be eligible for coverage.

PPO - Preferred Provider Organization
A type of health plan where you pay less if you use providers in
the plan's network. You can use doctors, hospitals, and
providers outside of the network without a referral for an
additional cost.

POS - Point of Service
A type of plan where you pay less if you use doctors, hospitals, and other
health care providers that belong to the plan's network.

EPO - Exclusive Provider Organization
Services are covered only if you use doctors, specialists, or
hospitals in the plan's network (except in an emergency).

High Deductible Health Plan – HDHP
A plan with a higher deductible than a traditional insurance plan. The
monthly premium is usually lower, but you pay more health care costs
yourself before the insurance company starts to pay its share (your
deductible). A high deductible plan (HDHP) can be combined with a
health savings account (HSA), allowing you to pay for certain medical
expenses with money free from federal taxes.

Today, one of the more prevalent features used to evaluate our insurance
plan is whether or not the doctor participates in your plan. Therefore,
rather than get hung up on acronym or title of your health plan, take the
time to understand how your health plan works, what's covered, what
your financial responsibility is and what you may need to do to ensure

you get covered by your health plan.

Don't get misled or confused by health plan acronyms.
The abbreviations usually refer to an internal insurance company system to help manage the products. The codes can help to identify:
- State where the plan is licensed or operates
- Geographic region
- Market segment such as commercial, government, union
- Network of providers grouped together (limited network)
  Types of benefits or services offered

EXAMPLES OF HEALTH PLAN
NAMES AND CODES

	○ Open Choice® PPO
	○ Managed Choice® POS
	○ HMO
HMO	○ QPOS®
Cigna HealthCare of Connecticut, Inc. HMO	○ Aetna Affordable Health Choices® limited benefits insurance plan (SRC only)
Network, Network POS	
Seamless - Metro New York	○ Aetna Select℠
OAP	○ Aetna Voluntary Plans
Open Access Plus, OA plus, Choice Fund OA Plus	Aetna Open Access Plans
PPO	○ Aetna Choice® POS II (Open Access)
PPO, Choice Fund PPO	○ Aetna Health Network Only℠ (Open Access)
	○ Aetna Health Network Option℠ (Open Access)
	○ Aetna Select℠ (Open Access)
	○ Elect Choice® EPO (Open Access)
	○ Managed Choice® POS (Open Access)
	○ North Carolina State Health Plan - Effective 2015

Insurance network will determine where you get services

When we need to use healthcare services, those of us with health insurance typically have to make a choice about how we access such services.

When we get sick or need health care services, the natural inclination is to think about who can help us. Do you call your primary care doctor or fill a prescription? We just want to get well.

ACCESSING THE US HEALTHCARE SYSTEM

Patient's point of view

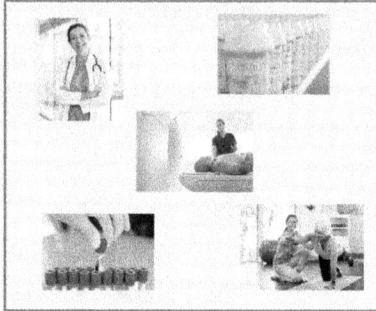

For most of us, being able to finance our healthcare services is a driving force with whether or how we seek treatment. In-network providers typically agree to how much they can charge you, or what the upper limit may be for a service. This can help minimize your out-of-pocket costs. Your health insurance plan design will also drive how much you would owe for such services, or how much you may be reimbursed. That's why access to healthcare services often starts with our health insurance. From there, we need to know which providers are in-network which determines how claims will get paid.

In-Network

Access to health care		Healthcare Delivery	Financial	

Health Insurance Company	⇨	Health Insurance Plan / Product	⇨	Healthcare systems Hospitals Doctors Healthcare Providers	⇨	Health Insurance Plan / Product	⇨	Claims paid to provider ⬇ You pay balance if applicable
		HMO PPO POS EPO Other						

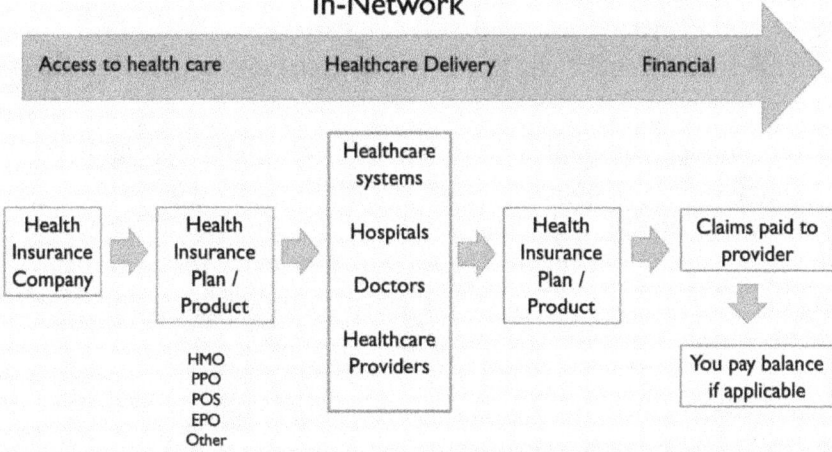

If you decide to go out-of-network, you just need to be aware of the process to get reimbursed from your health insurance company and understand what your true financial obligations may be. You are typically responsible to pay the full, billed amount to the provider up front. Then, you can seek reimbursement from your health insurance company.

Out-of-Network

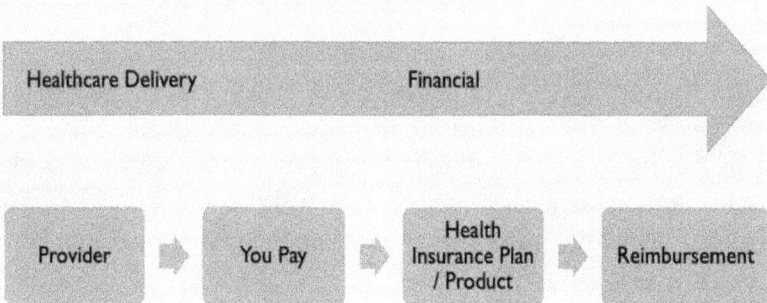

Healthcare Delivery		Financial	

Provider	⇨	You Pay	⇨	Health Insurance Plan / Product	⇨	Reimbursement

What exactly do health insurance companies do?

Health insurance companies perform a number of strategic and operational roles that support health care in the United States. One could say health insurance companies are an integral part of the fabric of the healthcare system with a primary focus of financing the payment of healthcare services, but also striving to provide higher quality of care.

As a consumer of health care, and heavily reliant upon insurance companies to facilitate the financing our health care services whether in part or in whole, it's important we understand what health insurance companies do in order to manage our expectations. While this book is not intended to be an exhaustive description of what health insurance companies do, here are four of the main components they deliver on that may help put their role into perspective.

1. Health insurance companies build and maintain a network of providers and services. In addition to contracting with medical and health providers like primary care doctors, specialists and hospitals, they also curate pharmacy networks and services.

   By participating in a health plan network, providers help with the financing aspects of health care and deliver on certain administrative tasks that streamline the process:
   - Agree to discounted rates
   - File claims on your behalf
   - Maintain quality and service standards

2. Perform claims processing and claims review activities:
   - Receive claim submissions via multiple methods including Electronically, mail, and by fax (yes, providers still use fax)
   - Timely adjudication of claims
   - Process claims per benefit plan design
   - Pay providers or members
   - Provide visibility to claims processed online or by paper

3. Deliver on a number of medical management activities that fosters quality health care:
   - Establish / define standards for what types of procedures & tests to cover through the plan
   - Manage authorization or pre-approval process for medical procedures
   - Coordination of health services
   - Wellness coaching
   - Disease management
   - Centers of Excellence (i.e., cancer, heart)
   - Provide Health information

4. Provide customer service
   - Answer questions by phone, chat, e-mail
   - Handle appeals
   - Send letters, correspondence
   - Provide digital experience: access to claims, tools, health information
   - Integration with health savings accounts
   - Behind the scenes: Data integration with multiple computer/technology systems

Evaluating Your Options

What kind of health plan makes sense for me?

It is not uncommon to have more than one health option to choose from. The easy choice may be to select the plan that costs us the least when we visit a doctor. On the surface, that could seem like the right choice. Consider my example of Ted in the introduction section who had an HMO plan that his wife loved; she was unaware of how much was being deducted from Ted's paycheck.

Why not find the right plan that meets your needs and is also the most cost-effective plan? What does cost-effective mean to you? Some people are willing to pay more in payroll contributions or monthly premiums to have lower deductibles; predictability of their payroll cash flow may be more manageable. They may also have limited savings in the bank to cover something catastrophic, so they need a plan that will cover health expenses without requiring a significant cost-sharing through the plan design.

You may be relatively healthy with a low expectation of needing health insurance. As a result, you want your payroll deductions to be minimized while providing most comprehensive coverage in case of a catastrophic health incident. Whichever way you slice it, the decision is a financial one. Therefore, selecting your medical insurance will be based on how much money it will cost you through:

- Payroll or Monthly Premiums
- Deductibles, Coinsurance, and Copays
- Plan Design Features

Payroll Contributions or Monthly Premiums to cover your share of the insurance:

If you're getting insurance through your employer, you're most likely contributing a portion of the total premium for the insurance through payroll contributions. This amount can range anywhere from 0% of the premium to 50% of the premium. Educational institutions, unions, and governmental agencies have a reputation to require a low employee contribution towards the cost of insurance. Small employer groups or employers in certain industries may pass on a higher portion of the premium cost to employees.

If you're getting insurance on the open market, you may be paying a monthly premium to the insurance company which isn't subsidized by an employer or other organization.

Plan Deductibles, Coinsurance, and Copay Levels:

Deductibles are the first-dollar responsibility of a covered member before the insurance plan starts to pay. A flat dollar amount of $250, $500, $1,000, $1,500 or higher are examples of deductible levels. Non- preventive services are usually applied to the deductible, along with pharmacy costs in certain types of medical plans. You may also see two different deductible levels: In-Network and Out-of-Network deductible levels. This applies when you seek services from a doctor who may or may not be in the network of an insurance company.

It is customary for amounts met toward an In-Network deductible to be also applied or given credit toward the Out-of-Network deductible. For example, say you have an In-Network deductible of $1,000 and an Out-of-Network deductible of

$2,000, and you receive $1,000 worth of approved medical services from an In-Network provider. You've met the In-Network deductible, and also received a $1,000 credit toward your Out-of-Network deductible.

Coinsurance is the amount you're responsible to pay after the insurance company makes its plan payment. For example, your coinsurance may be 10% for In-Network services, while the insurance company will pay 90% of the approved charges. Insurance plans have a feature called the **Maximum Coinsurance Limit**. This is the point at which the plan will actually pay out at 100% and the coinsurance level no longer applies. This is an excellent member specific benefit that minimizes your potential out- of-pocket costs in the event you experience a very significant amount of health care costs in a given year. For example, if your coinsurance maximum limit is $2,000, usually you meet the deductible first at $1,000, then have to pay another $1,000 in coinsurance. When you add up the 10%s you pay each time, once it meets $1,000, you've met your coinsurance maximum limit.

The coinsurance maximum is a relatively unknown or ambiguous insurance concept that doesn't get a lot of press. Simply, it's the point at which your medical plan will pay 100% of covered expenses.

When claims first come in, they get applied toward your deductible. Once you meet your deductible, the insurance will start paying on claims at 70%, 80% or 90%, depending on what the plan design says. You're liable for the 10%, 20% or 30%. Adding up the coinsurance amounts will then get you to your coinsurance maximum at which point the plan will pay at 100%.

Illustration of Total Contributions Made (single coverage)

	Plan A	Plan B	Plan C
Annual Payroll Contributions	$2,000	$1,200	$800
Annual Deductible	$1000	$2,000	$3,000
Coinsurance Maximum	$2000	$2,000	$3,000
Total	$5,000	$5,200	$6,800

Plan Design Features
Look Beyond the Immediate Plan Costs

Medical plans offered by employers (and even the ones offered through the Marketplace) offer a common core or minimum set of benefits and services. The Affordable Care Act and a number of state insurance laws have made that possible. More consistency and minimum standards exist across plans. The Affordable Care Act requires most people to have health care coverage that qualifies as minimum essential coverage.

But variations still exist.

Some plans cover more than the minimum requirements, and others do not. It all depends on what type of plan was purchased either by your employer, group plan, or through the open market. For group health plans through your employer, variations can exist based upon the state your plan is based in.

If your plan is fully-insured, it must follow state insurance guidelines for benefits covered. If the plan is self-insured, it does not have to follow state insurance guidelines; rather self-insured plans must include at least the minimum essential coverage, and then may cover certain categories of richer benefits, such as covering a higher number of physical therapy visits or provide a different dollar value benefit for infertility.

Some plans require more cost-sharing features or have limitations on how many visits or dollar amounts are covered in a given calendar year or even a lifetime.

Here are some examples of plan design features to watch out for:

- Hospital fee if admitted overnight, in addition to other plan deductible/coinsurance fees

- Prescription costs applied against your plan deductible first, along with medical costs, before the plan pays out Maximum number of short-term rehabilitation visits for physical, speech, cognitive, and occupational therapy

- Maximum lifetime benefits for infertility services such as lab and radiology tests, counseling, surgical treatment, artificial insemination, and in-vitro fertilization

- Maximum copay or coinsurance amount paid for prescriptions

The Benefits Summary (also called the Summary of Benefits and Coverage) will itemize what's covered by benefit category, how it is covered, and any limitations or dollar values associated with that benefit. Therefore, understanding what your health care needs are, or may be, is critical to mapping out what to expect from your health plan. Researching how items are covered is part of your due diligence in knowing your benefits.

Repeat: The Summary of Benefits and Coverage may be one of the most important plan documents to read (in addition to a Summary Plan Description).

To help consumers compare the different features of health benefits and coverage, the Affordable Care Act generally requires all group health plans and health insurance companies to provide individuals a "summary of benefits and coverage" that "accurately describes the benefits and coverage under the plan." Visit the CMS.gov website to learn more and view a sample of an SBC.

https://marketplace.cms.gov/technical-assistanceresources/summary-of-benefits-fast-facts.pdf

https://www.cms.gov/CCIIO/Resources/Forms-Reports-and-Other- Resources/Downloads/Sample-Completed-SBC-Accessible- Format01-2020.pdf

Reading an Explanation of Benefits (EOB) Statement

The EOB is the official explanation on how an insurer paid your claim. The EOB identifies what, if anything, you may owe a doctor or health care provider. Most doctor offices are able to file claims electronically, and given how cash flow is king, they will file in a very timely fashion in order to get paid. Doctors may send you an invoice for anything owed, even if the insurance company hasn't processed or paid the claim yet.

Be proactive and check EOBs online timely (within a few weeks after your doctor visit). Get ahead of any doctor billing statements that are set to arrive in your mailbox. Know what to expect in terms of amounts due. Doctors usually expect you to pay them within a net 30-day period. Therefore, when the doctor bills you, be ready to know whether what they say you owe is accurate.

Can you tell what you owe a health care professional from reading an EOB statement?

When a health claim is submitted and processed by your insurance company, they will produce a claims or payment summary called an Explanation of Benefits or EOB for short. The EOB illustrates a number of features, including one most important one: What you owe the health care professional.

To understand what you may owe, you should become familiar with the different components of the EOB. The following **Claim detail** is a simple example of a preventive claim paid at 100% by the insurance carrier.

In this example, after submitting their charge, the health care professional's fees were discounted or reduced by $35.67 as the initial charges were higher than the negotiated rate, leaving $49.33 as the covered amount. Since this claim was preventive in nature and the provider was In-Network, the plan paid 100% of the covered amount directly to the health care professional.

Explanation of Benefits Claim Detail

Claim detail

received this claim on December 8, 2016 and processed it on December 9, 2016.

Service dates	Type of service	Amount billed	Discount	Amount not covered	Covered amount	Copay/ Deductible	What your plan paid	% paid	Coinsurance*	See notes
12/07/16	IMMUNIZATIONS	45.00	26.16	0.00	18.84	0.00	18.84	100	0.00	A0
12/07/16	IMMUNIZATIONS	40.00	9.51	0.00	30.49	0.00	30.49	100	0.00	A0
Total		$85.00	$35.67	$0.00	$49.33	$0.00	$49.33		$0.00	

Claim Subject to Deductible

If you did not meet your deductible, you will owe money to the health care professional. In the following example, a procedure was performed that cost $865.00. However, the In-Network discount was applied reducing the fee to $141.69. After the discount is applied, the claim gets processed, taking into account your Plan Design features, and whether you met your deductible. In this example, the patient did not meet their deductible. However, the patient only owed $141.69, the negotiated rate for the procedure. The insurance company even made a comment about this feature in the Notes section. This is a great example as to why you want to wait for your health insurance company to process the claim before you even consider paying your health care professional.

Explanation of Benefits: Applied to Deductible

Service(s) From: 10/11/2016 • To: 10/11/2016   Customize My View ▦

Service Date & Type	Amount Billed	Discount	Amount Not Covered	Covered Amount	Copay / Deductible	What Your Plan Paid	Coinsurance	What I Owe	See Notes
10/11/2016 •	$865.00	$723.31	$0.00	$141.69	$141.69	0% = $0.00	$0.00	$141.69	0248
TOTALS	$865.00	$723.31	$0.00	$141.69	$141.69	$0.00	$0.00	$141.69	

Notes
0248 - $723.31 The discount shown is how much you saved. You don't need to pay that amount. If you already paid your health care professional more than the "What I Owe" amount, please ask for a refund.

Understand what you owe when your doctor sends you a bill

Health care professionals are in business to make money. Yes, they are there to help people get or stay healthy. But, at the end of the day, health care is a profession that employs people which carries costs of doing business such as paying salaries, buying office equipment, leasing office space, paying malpractice insurance, etc.

Medical professionals enlist the services of well-trained billing and coding professionals whose sole job is to maximize cash flow for the health care business or, basically, collect the debts owed by patients who received health care treatment.

It's not uncommon to be asked to make a payment when you are in your health care professional's office. If the provider is In-Network, you may be asked to make a co-payment toward your office visit based upon a conversation the billing department had with your insurance company in advance of your arrival. From their conversation with the insurance company, they may be able to estimate what you may might owe, but it won't be accurate.

Ideally, you want to wait until after the office visit is completed and the health care professional actually submitted a claim to your insurance carrier for processing. Why is this important? Well, your doctor may not know the full extent of what tests and procedures he/she needed to do until you were actually examined. Let the insurance company do their thing and identify what you owe as illustrated in the EOB. What if you paid too much? You would need to then wait for a refund. Why give them your money upfront if you don't have to?

Let the insurance company notify the health care professional first on how the claim was processed. At that time, you'll be billed for what you truly owe. You can ask the health care professional for a summary statement of what procedures were performed at the time of the visit. Compare the health care professional's invoice against the EOB. Do they match up? The invoice will list the insurance company discounts, possibly as write-offs. Look for negative amounts on the invoice to reflect the discounted amounts made by the insurance carrier.

Explanation of Benefits (EOB) Terms Defined

Amount billed: The amount charged by the health care professional or facility (physician, hospital, etc.) for services provided to you or your covered dependents.

Amount not covered: The portion of the amount billed that was not covered or eligible for payment under your plan. Examples include charges for services or products that are not covered by your plan, duplicate claims that are not your responsibility and any charges submitted that are above the maximum amount your plan pays for out- of-network care.

Deductible: The portion of submitted charges applied towards your deductible. Your deductible is the amount you need to pay each year before your plan starts paying benefits.

Copay: A flat fee you pay for certain covered services such as doctor visits or prescriptions.

Discount: The amount you save by using a health care professional or facility (doctor, hospital, etc.) that belongs to the insurance network. Insurance company negotiates lower rates with its in- network doctors, hospitals and other facilities to help you save money.

In-Network: A group of health care professionals and facilities (doctors, hospitals, labs, etc.) that offer discounts on services based on their relationship with the insurance company. Using in-network services gives you significant discounts, which help you stretch your health care account money further.

Out-of-Network: Health care professionals and facilities (doctors, hospitals, labs, etc.) that do not belong to the insurance network.
Depending on your plan, you can use out-of-network services, but you may pay more for the same services, and you might have to file a separate claim for reimbursement.

What your plan paid: The portion of the billed amount that was paid by your health care plan. The balance of that amount is your responsibility. This amount might include your deductible, coinsurance, any amount over the maximum reimbursable charge, or products or services not covered by your plan.

Be an Active Consumer of Your Health Insurance

There is no secret answer, silver bullet, or shortcut toward getting the most from your health insurance. You have to cast a wide net and keep your eyes open for those opportunities. Not everyone may uncover financial savings, but if you're not paying attention, you'll likely miss them. Based upon my professional and personal experience, as well as research into this topic, here are a number of key strategies and actions you can start doing now to take control of your health insurance.

Register online with your plan right away

All too often we need to access/use our health insurance plans when we're in a crunch or it's an emergency-like situation: you need an ID card or have to fill a prescription. You may need to know how much is left in your health savings account or have a need to download a claim form. It's at that point you're scrambling and don't know what to do. You send an e-mail or call your benefits specialist at work and wait for a response.

Take a few minutes when you first enroll to log onto your online account with the health plan and familiarize yourself with the types of features and actions available through the online portal:

o Familiarize yourself with how to access your account. A website address or URL is typically what you need. Navigate around to find out what resources, tools and forms are available. Often these sites offer a brief, recorded tutorial highlighting how to best use the site

- Use the site map as a shortcut to find online resources; a site map is comparable to a table of contents or an index to all of the website's pages without the banners, icons, images and other Web page graphics
- Update your personal preferences such as your e-mail and account settings. This is important as you can edit your document delivery preferences: paper or online; choose the type of notifications to receive and when such as when a claim is processed and paid
- Learn how to order additional ID Cards, if needed, including temporary/electronic versions you can save to your PC, print or e- mail to yourself/family members for future use
- Download the insurance company app to your mobile device. Apps now can give you instant access to all of the basic, important information such as your ID number, claims, doctor searches, and covered benefits
- Review your insurance coverage
- Look up claims payments and statements
- Find a doctor or facility that is In-Network
- Order home delivery of your prescriptions
- Estimate costs of health care
- Verify enrollment on yourself and any covered family members
- Complete a Health Risk Assessment or Health Questionnaire
- Access health resources to research health topics, and/or treatment options

Download the insurance plan's mobile app from AppStore or Google Play as many, if not all, of the same features available online can be accessed via the plan's mobile app.

Don't pay up front for medical visits, even if a co-payment is required.

This one is probably one of my top pet peeves. You may be asked to pay a doctor upon leaving the office, after your visit. How do they know what you owe? They may say they've estimated based upon prior claims processed. Or they've called the insurance company to verify what your deductible is and how much you owe.

This doesn't always mean what they say you owe is or will be what you owe. Don't pay up front. Wait for the insurance company to process the claim and issue an EOB. Several reasons to do this:

If In-Network, you should never pay up front. Maybe, if you know you have a $20 office visit co-pay, you probably should, but even then, if it's a preventive visit, you might not owe anything as preventive care In-Network is covered at 100%.

You want the insurance company to process the claim, apply any discounts or negotiated rates, apply against your deductible (if not met) and pay according to the plan design (i.e., 80% or 90% after deductible). Then you know for sure what you owe. You could have other claims being processed which can impact the outcome of the current doctor's claim.

Negotiated rates can vary by plan and by insurance group. The rate for a procedure or test can be different across plans. The U.S. government healthcare website defines usual, customary and reasonable as being "The amount paid for a medical service in a geographic area based on what providers in the area usually charge for the same or similar medical service. The UCR amount sometimes is used to determine the allowed amount."

A doctor or medical facility will bill you or your insurance company in an itemized manner. An office visit, test, lab work, injections, for example, are all coded individually and carry a different charge. Some procedures are actually grouped together and shouldn't be unbundled. This adds to the overall charge amount but can impact the final amount considered by the insurance company which, in turn, can also impact what you owe. And if you're In-Network, the doctor needs to accept whatever claims adjudication occurs. Unless the doctor informs you up front that a procedure will not be covered at all and gets your agreement to perform it and that you'll be responsible for it, you are not responsible for a charge if deemed uncovered by the insurance company. Check the codes on the EOB statement

Your medical plan benefits can change from one year to the next. You may have paid a certain co-pay or coinsurance amount in a prior year or through another employer. Your doctor's office may not have the latest information on your plan benefits, and are working off old information

Like any professional service offered, payment for such services should be made in an agreed upon time frame. Businesses, such as medical providers, usually expect payment within 30 days from their patients. Beyond that, the provider may extend payment terms to 60 or 90 days before you are sent to collections. Your provider should provide you with written terms on their billing practices which could include terms on when they start to charge you interest on balances due

Remember, medical expenses account for approximately 62% of personal bankruptcies in the United States. Learn how to keep more of your money in your pocket

Learn in advance what CPT codes will be billed

The **Current Procedural Terminology (CPT)** code set is a medical code maintained by the American Medical Association through the CPT Editorial Panel.[1] The CPT code set (copyright protected by the AMA) describes medical, surgical, and diagnostic services and is designed to communicate uniform information about medical services and procedures among physicians, coders, patients, accreditation organizations, and payors for administrative, financial, and analytical purposes.

There are CPT codes representing hundreds, if not thousands, of different medical procedures for all types of medical conditions. For example, codes in the range of 99201 through 99215 represent office visits and other outpatient services. The CPT code and a diagnosis, along with patient information, dates of service and provider information are used when submitting a claim to an insurance carrier for payment.

You can ask for these from your doctor's office and your insurance company to verify if the CPT is covered and/or how much is covered. Many online health insurance portals have a tool where you can enter the CPT codes or procedure names which tell you if covered, and what the contracted or approved rate may be for your plan. Then, you would need to apply whatever financial plan design features exist, such as deductible, coinsurance, copay, In- or Out-of-network.

Find out in advance, if possible, what CPT codes your medical professionals will be performing on you and then research with your insurance company how those codes are covered.

Read the Summary of Benefits and Coverage

The Summary of Benefits and Coverage (SBC) is a plan document that tells you the story about your insurance plan including what's covered and how things are covered. Usually, an insurance company follows a standard template format to display plan benefits.

The SBC is typically produced annually for each contract or plan year. Therefore, it's important you get a copy annually. The format of SBCs follows a template created by the Centers for Medicare and Medicaid Services (CMS) which can be found on the CMS website:

https://www.cms.gov/CCIIO/Resources/Forms-Reports-and-OtherResources/Downloads/Sample-Completed-SBC-Accessible- Format01-2020.pdf

While the CMS version of the SBC has a minimum set of data points in their template, your health insurance plan may also produce their own Benefits Summary for your particular health plan that goes into more detail including items that are excluded. Having a Benefit Summary in your possession will keep you informed and prevent any surprises down the road after a claim is paid, especially if you find out you actually owe more money than you thought.

Benefit Summaries identify the financial components you may be responsible for such as annual deductibles and coinsurance maximum limits. The Summary will describe coverage information by categories such as Preventive, Physician

Services, In-Patient, Pharmacy, Mental Health, and Other Services. Additionally, you'll find a list of non-covered or excluded items along with special programs and ancillary services covered such as wellness, care management, and specialty pharmacy management. Definition of terms may also be listed.

Don't assume just because your doctor says you need it that it's covered

A doctor's office is a business.

Doctors have hundreds if not thousands of patients (customers) so how can you expect them to know the details of your specific plan?

Doctor's offices are not experts in insurance. They rely upon office staff dedicated to financial matters to handle insurance claims.

All insurance plans are not alike which is why you need to become an expert on your own plan.

Denied claims also contribute to medical bill problems among those with insurance. About a quarter (26%) of the insured who had medical bill problems say they had a claim denied by their insurance company. Common reported reasons for denial include a particular treatment not being covered (25% of those with denied claims) and receiving care from an Out-of-Network provider (14%); 21% of those who say they had a claim denied did not know or could not provide a reason for the denial.[2]

Save a copy of your enrollment confirmation statement

When you make a benefit election, it's important to obtain a hard copy or electronic version of your elections. This would be a confirmation of your benefit elections for the current or upcoming plan year. Often these statements include the date of your election.

Most online benefit election systems automatically produce a confirmation statement whether by e-mail, in PDF, or other form which you can then print or save to your computer. If you submit your benefit elections on a paper election form, you should expect to receive a confirmation statement in a timely basis, within 30 days or less. You may be advised to go online to produce this statement.

A confirmation statement of your benefit elections is important for a number of reasons:

- Confirms what you elected for the current or upcoming plan year
- Identifies what you should be paying for such coverage
- Lists all dependents enrolled in each of the benefit plans covered

In the event of a discrepancy, you can show your confirmation statement to your employer or other group plan administrator. Use the confirmation statement as proof of your payroll contributions when reviewing your first paycheck of the new plan year to verify that your employer is deducting the right amount of money. The confirmation statement can also be used to verify your enrollment in each of the health plans to your employer.

System glitches do happen, so you need to be prudent in keeping good records of proof of your benefit elections. Having such proof will only make any requests to clarify or correct discrepancies easier.

Have a system to track your claims and insurance payments

Keeping it simple is always a practical approach. Having a system will also help you feel more in control.

Open all bills. I know it can be unpleasant to review your bills, especially if you're not sure if you really owe the money.

Organize by status, such as Paid, Need to Pay and Waiting on Insurance to Pay First.

Review your bills at the same time each month. Having a system to stay organized is crucial.

Keep notes like you would a diary or a log of activity about any open bills. If you're waiting on your doctor's office to respond to you as to why you're being billed, write down the day you called, who you spoke to and when they will be calling you back. Then schedule in advance a date when you will follow up.

Dedicate a place in your house for insurance stuff, perhaps keep with your regular bills or a section nearby. You need a way to keep track of your insurance bills. Tossing them into a box or corner isn't a solution.

Use notebooks, file folders, accordion folders, and file pockets and jackets, or other organizing resources. Keep it organized by family member as well as by calendar year. If you don't, after a while, the paper will accumulate, and it'll become overwhelming.

How long should you keep copies of your bills and paperwork? Rule of thumb may be to follow five to seven years in case you're audited on your taxes, but you can decide what the likelihood of that may be.

Consider taking the generic over the name brand prescription

According to Wikipedia, a **generic drug** is a pharmaceutical drug that is equivalent to a brand-name product in dosage, strength, route of administration, quality, performance, and intended use. The term may also refer to any drug marketed under its chemical name without advertising, or to the chemical makeup of a drug rather than the brand name under which the drug is sold.

Generic drugs in the United States are subject to government regulations, and as such must contain the same active ingredients as the original brand-name formulation. The US Food and Drug Administration (FDA) requires that generics be identical to, or within an acceptable bioequivalent range of, their brand-name counterparts with respect to their pharmacokinetic properties.

Essentially and legally, a generic must have the same drug ingredients of a name brand drug with the same intended effect, *but at a lesser cost.*

Generics become available because the patent of the name brand expires, permitting other pharmaceutical companies to create and sell the generic version of the brand drug formula.

The Association for Accessible Medicines, an industry group that promotes generics and biosimilar, reports that 90% of the all the prescriptions dispensed are generic and biosimilar prescriptions, but that they only account for 13.1% of the prescription drug spend in the United States [3]. Dispensed is an industry term that basically means "issued by a pharmacy". The dispensing could be through a retail pharmacy, mail order, a hospital system or some other outpatient method.

Why Should I consider Generics over a Brand Name Prescription?

A popular name brand prescription called Lipitor, used to lower cholesterol in adults and some children, saw the introduction of its generic equivalent, Atorvastatin, in 2010. Immediately, the generic version resulted in a 97% price-reduction compared to the pre-generic cost of Lipitor.[4] This translates directly into the pocket of the consumer. Patient co-payments were drastically reduced. These types of price reductions are common when a brand name drug becomes generic.

Prescription benefits often include a tiered approach when it comes to your co-pay or financial contribution towards prescriptions. You may see two, three or even four tiers of plan design levels with each tier corresponding to a different level of insurance coverage. You may see the tiers broken into preventive, generic and name brand. Even further splintering may occur, such as preventive generics, and name-brand with or without a generic equivalent.

Preventive Drugs

The Affordable Care Act requires that preventive generic drugs be covered at 100%, with no out-of-pocket costs for the patient enrolled in a medical plan. If the prescription is a brand name preventive drug, you may find a low copayment, such as $10 or only 10% coinsurance level required by the patient. The preventive prescription is also NOT subject to the plan deductible. Keep in mind this could change beyond depending on what the U.S. Federal Government passes as law. Visit following website to learn more.
https://www.uspreventiveservicestaskforce.org/

Generics

Prescriptions are in this category of drugs when the name brand is no longer exclusive, and typically carry a significantly lower patient cost when purchasing through your pharmacy benefit. Non- preventive generic drugs may be subject to a plan deductible, but the cost of the drug is dramatically lower than its name-brand colleague.

Incentives to Use Generics

Commercial insurance, Medicare, Medicaid and other payors benefit from using generics. For example, a 2016 GAO report found that prices for generic drugs in Medicare Part D declined 59% from the first quarter of 2010 to the second quarter of 2015 saving the Medicare program (and the people enrolled) money. Nevertheless, pharmaceutical cost is the fastest growing segment of health care, ranging from 15 up to 20% of the total cost of health care. Given that generics cost significantly less than their name brand counterparts, insurance payors would stand to benefit from an increased number of generics being dispensed.

Marketplace methods to encourage the use of generics

Receive your generics prescription for free a period of time. If you take a maintenance prescription drug month after month, you may be eligible to receive your prescription for free for a trial period through the insurance company as a way to introduce you to the generic version.

The hope is after a six-month trial period, you'll be happy using the generic and will decide to continue using it. The results of such plan designs to encourage the use of converting to a generic drug are mixed, and unlikely will result in complete conversion.

Increased costs if you fill with a name brand when a generic is available. The plan design may carry a higher copayment or coinsurance rate if you choose to fill with the name brand drug. Some plans may include a mandatory generic that penalizes you for not only the patient cost of the name brand, but also the cost-differential between the name brand and generic.

Physicians may receive financial incentives, legally, to prescribe generics.[5] Pharmaceutical companies may give physicians free samples to hand out to their patients to try a generic which may have the same effect as a name brand. Also, physicians may receive financial or monetary incentives from payors or pharmaceutical companies to prescribe generics. While the incentive may not be direct compensation for prescribing generics, the reward may come in a form of incentives for reducing overall pharmacy costs for their patients.[6]

Why Some People Don't Like Using Generic Drugs
While the cost may be an attractive component to using a generic drug, people who are used to taking a name brand drug that has worked just fine are cautious to switch, and for good reason.

A drug has both active and inactive ingredients. Next time you're at a retail pharmacy, compare the ingredients of a generic form of most over-the-counter item, such as a nasal spray, foot crème or ibuprofen. You'll notice that the active ingredients are typically identical.

A Few Words about Drug Coupons

A **drug coupon** is a coupon intended to help consumers save money on prescription drugs. Distributed to consumers through doctors, pharmacists or online, drug coupons are available for drugs from many categories such as cholesterol, acne, migraines, allergies, and other medical conditions. Unfortunately, generic drug companies rarely offer coupons.

Drug manufacturers have offered discount coupon programs more in recent years, in part because insurance companies often charge consumers higher co-pays for brand-name products. The offers can be enticing. Indeed, nearly 16%, or nearly 19 million, of all Americans who regularly take a prescription medication have used coupons according to a 2011 survey by the Consumer Reports National Research Center.[7]

Be careful, though. Getting hooked on prescription-drug coupons may not be the bargain they claim to be. Consumer Reports examined drug coupons and advised on a number of points based upon their research you should be aware of:

"Do the math"
Is using the drug coupon the least-cost option? Consider using a generic which is usually a low-cost option. Some insurance plans exclude the use of coupons, so by not following the

rules of your plan, you may be impacting yourself.

"Avoid imitations"
Make sure you get the actual prescription you need, in the right dosage and quantity.

"Watch for limitations"
The coupon may only be good for a few months or available based upon a limited supply.

"Consider the long term"
The coupons lower your costs, but not those of your insurance company. In the end, your plan may experience higher prescription costs in the aggregate, and thereby pass on cost increases next year through higher payroll contributions.

Prescription Mail Order

Most insurance plans offer a program where they can mail you a longer supply of prescription drugs at a reduced price. For example, you may get three-month supply for the cost of two months, a 3 for 2 deal. But be careful to make sure it's the best deal for you.

Mail order pharmacy programs operate through your insurer's pharmacy benefit manager, or PBM. The companies—CVS Caremark, Express Scripts, and others—buy medications in bulk directly from drug manufacturers, and by doing so, can translate to lower co-pay charges for some of your medications. That's especially true for drugs you might take on a regular basis for conditions such as diabetes or high blood pressure. You could get a 90-day supply of generic medication sent directly to your home with co-pays that run just a few dollars or are even free, compared to a discounted $10 copay for a three-month prescription at your local drugstore.[8]

Some insurance plans or PBMs now allow you to get the same 90-day supply at retail instead of ordering through the mail for certain classes of drugs.

What are the downsides of using Mail order?

Auto-renew

Your prescription may re-order itself automatically. This is a feature you sign-up for when you first submit your order. There may be an opt-in feature signing you up for auto-renew. Opt-in means you're enrolled in the program and must actively sign up to NOT receive a renewal automatically. This feature is convenient as it streamlines your order. However, if you've made plans to obtain the prescription elsewhere or no longer need it, you'll end up with paying additional fees.

Less personal

People like the personal touch when obtaining their medications, especially if they have a personal relationship with their pharmacist. Going mail-order may eliminate your ability to ask questions.

Risk of damaged, lost or stolen prescriptions

As with any shipments ordered online, you're dependent upon the delivery system to bring your package to your house in one piece and on time. FedEx, USPS and other services are fairly reliable, but risk still exist. A number of factors can prevent your item from arriving as needed. Are you comfortable taking the chance of a medication not arriving? If mishaps arise, you can contact the insurance company to rectify the order, but it will only delay you receiving your completed order.

Extra work to submit and manage your order

Mail-order prescriptions can be fulfilled online or by the telephone. Either you or your doctor can submit the prescription online, or you can mail it in directly to the insurance company. This requires you to complete paperwork, answer questions online, and submit credit card information to guarantee payment even if you have insurance in place. Some people don't like the administrative burden associated with mail- order.

Drug Discount Programs through Big Chain Stores

While my book if focused on maximizing your health insurance, I do want to point out an alternative to filling your prescriptions that may save you money.

A number of national retail stores like Costco, Walmart Walgreen's, Rite Aid, Sam's Club and Publix Supermarket are offering lower cost prescription drugs through their own drugstore and pharmacy discount drug programs which may prove less expensive than using your prescription drug coverage through your health plan.

Essentially, these programs are offering a discount on the cash price of prescriptions when you don't use your prescription insurance.

Negotiate to apply any deductibles met with your prior plan to your new plan if you change mid-year

Health insurance companies will start the clock on calculating your deductible credit from the day you start new with an insurance policy. There isn't some magical insurance fairy who knows that you may have already met some or all of your medical plan deductible in a plan.

If you change medical plans in the middle of the year and not during the normal open enrollment period, you may be able to negotiate to have any amount met toward your deductible from your prior plan transferred over to the new plan. This may not be a standard practice, but certainly a feasible one that I've seen done.

Obtain the latest insurance EOB (explanation of benefits) for each and every family member which reflects your year-to-date deductible and coinsurance totals. Every EOB that gets produced will have this accumulated tally on it, so if you produce the latest claims paid, you should be good. This statement can usually be downloaded to a PDF, as well, so save a copy.

Two options to pursue:

-Ask your employer's benefits resource to advocate for you. They usually have a dedicated insurance account representative who can navigate the insurance company system internally.

-Contact the insurance company directly by phone first to ask how you can get your prior plan deductible reviewed and applied to your new insurance account. At first, the customer service representative may respond in doubt or even say no initially.

Persist. Ask to speak with a claims supervisor or manager if they are unable or not sure what to do.

Ultimately, you will need to mail it into the insurance company for review. You'll need to create a simple cover letter requesting that they honor your prior plan deductible. The letter could look something like this:

Date
Re: First and Last Name (your name)
      Insurance ID #
      Application of Prior Plan Deductible

Amounts Dear Insurance:

I recently enrolled in the (name of insurance company) on (effective date) through my employer (name if applicable). Before this effective date, I was enrolled in another insurance plan where I met $ (insert amount) toward my annual deductible. Since I left that plan mid-year for personal/employment reasons (you don't have to explain why), I would appreciate your review to apply the deductible amount I met through my prior insurance company to my current insurance plan through (insert insurance name).

I've included a copy of a statement from my prior insurance plan which illustrates how much deductible I met. Here's a summary of what has been met:

Name (employee) $$$$ Name (spouse) $$$$
Thank you very much for your consideration. I'll look forward to your decision. I can be reached at (phone number).

Sincerely,

If you've had medical claims submitted prior to the insurance company giving you credit for your prior plan deductible amount, you may need to call them back to request they reprocess your claims.

Going In-Network is less expensive

Most people trust their doctor. It's hard to switch unless there's compelling reason to find a new doctor. Sometimes when we change health plans we're concerned as to whether our doctor is in the new insurance company's provider network. We may be forced to look for another doctor who is in the network for financial reasons.

There are a number of reasons why going In-Network may be more advantageous than seeking care on an Out-of-Network basis.

- In-Network providers agree to accept negotiated rates paid by insurance companies. While discounts are all over the place, In-Network rates are typically less than the original charged rate. If the In-Network doctor charges $500, but the negotiated rate is $200, you're only looking at $200 as an eligible charge. From there, your benefit plan design will apply the $200 towards your annual deductible and you'll only owe $200, not the full $500.

- If you go Out-of-Network, the insurance company will only apply their customary or maximum allowable rate toward your Out-of- Network deductible and maximum out-of-pocket calculations. If a doctor charges $850 for a procedure, but the insurance company maximum rate is $300, you'll only get credit for the $300.

- If you already met your deductible, the plan would pay the Out-of- Network reimbursement rate on the maximum allowable rate. For example, say the plan pays 60% on Out-of-Network claims, thcy would pay $180 (60% of $300), but you would still owe $670 ($850 minus $180).

- In-Network doctors understand how the insurance plan works. They will file claims directly on your behalf and may be in a position to advocate for you in case of appeals or claim payment discrepancies. Out-of-Network doctors typically do not want to be tied to any of the rules an insurance company may impose upon them.

- Question why a doctor isn't part of your insurance company's network. Did they apply but were not accepted? Or were they excluded for some reason?

- Staying In-network increases the chance that your health claims will be covered. According to a Kaiser Family Foundation survey[9], about three in 10 (32%) of those who had problems paying medical bills while insured say they received care from an Out-of-Network provider that their insurance wouldn't pay for. For many, these bills came as a surprise. Seven in 10 (69%) of those who had problems paying for care received from an Out-of-Network provider say they were unaware that the provider was not in their plan's network when they received the care.

While not every plan covers Out-of-Network care (except in emergency situations), it's important to understand the financial impact of going Out-of-Network in advance.

IN NETWORK	OUT OF NETWORK
The doctor bill is $825. Doctors in the network agree to a contracted price of $500 for the type of visit. This is all the doctor can collect. So you get a $325 discount at the start. **Your cost so far is $0.00**	The doctor bill is $825. The out-of-network "allowed amount for this type of visit is $400. The doctor can look to you to pay the rest, in this case $425. That amount is your responsibility and is called balance billing. **Your cost so far is $425**
You pay your deductible for network care which is $50 $500 less $50 leaves $450 **You cost so far is $50 ($0 + $50)**	You pay your deductible for out-of-network care, which is $100. Deductibles for out-of-network care are usually higher than for network care. $400 less $100 leaves $300 **Your cost so far is $525 ($425 + $100)**
Now that you've met your deductible, your plan pays 80% of the rest. In this case, that's $450. Your plan pays $360 (80% of $450). You pay the other 20% or $90. This amount is called your coinsurance. **Your total cost is $140 ($0 + $50 + $90)**	Now that you've met your deductible, your plan pays 60% of the remaining allowed amount. In this case, that's $300. Your plan pays $180 (60% of $300). You pay the other 40% or $120. This amount is called your coinsurance. Insurance pays a smaller percentage for out-of-network care than for network care. That means your coinsurance (the percentage you pay) is higher. **Your total cost is $645 ($425 + $100 + $120)**

Confirm Your Doctor is In-Network

Verify with the plan that your doctor is In-Network. The doctor may say they accept all insurance, but that doesn't equate to being in the plan network. Look them up on the insurance company Doctor Find tool. A physician's practice may be registered with the insurance company by their practice name. If the practice has more than one doctor, confirm whether other doctors participate or not. If your doctor is not listed, the practice may actually be in the network and bill using a different name for any claims.

Request your doctor join if not In-Network. A special request can be made for the doctor to participate in the network either on a provisionary or exclusive basis just for you or your situation. The doctor needs to initiate the process to apply which can take several months to complete, so plan ahead.

Pay with your credit card to earn points, then reimburse yourself from your health savings account

Why not earn points?

If you have a health savings account, this means you have a large deductible to meet, potentially $1,500, $2,000 or more. You know you'll owe this much money up front.

If you pay your doctor using your credit card, you get 30 days to float before you'll owe on the credit card. That gives you time to deduct money out of your health savings account at an ATM, or even request a check or transfer funds from the bank account that manages your health savings account which can be transferred over to your own bank account, and then pay your credit card timely. This is a little extra work, but if you bank electronically (like most people), this can help you earn additional savings and money. Check your credit card's reward program to learn how you earn points.

Review your employer paystub at least quarterly

96% of Americans are paid electronically through direct deposit from their employer. How many of those do you think actually review their paystub on a regular basis? I would venture to guess less than 5%.

Not only confirm you're getting paid correctly and having the right amount of taxes deducted but confirm what your insurance and benefit plan deductions are. If not accurate, this will give you ample time for Payroll/Benefits to adjust and refund you (if you over paid) or allow you time to catch up if you've under paid.

Contributions to your health savings account, flexible spending account, commuter benefit and many voluntary benefit plans are done through your payroll. Catching issues early saves time and money. If you find out in a subsequent tax year that something wasn't correct, there's a good chance you're out of luck as companies close the books on payroll once the tax year is over, and they don't like to reissue adjusted W-2s. Plus, many benefit plans are tied to the calendar year and won't allow you to make adjustments after the fact in a new tax year.

True Life Example: Your sole dependent child turned age 26 in May. According to plan rules, they have to leave the plan at the end of the month they turn 26. This changed the coverage tier from Family coverage to Associate plus One, altering how much you pay towards health coverage. However, the coverage tier didn't change in the HR/Payroll system, so you've continued to pay the higher payroll contribution amount. If this isn't caught in the current tax year, you probably won't get refunded.

Keep More Money in Your Pocket

Pre-tax as much as you can

Reducing your taxable wage not only reduces the amount of tax you pay, but also increases your net pay. This seems counterintuitive, but essentially for every dollar you reduce your wages by, you are saving on average about 27%.

For employees who obtain their health insurance through their job, take advantage of contributing as much as you can through regular payroll.

Most of us have this option anyway but be sure you're covering the right dependents on the plan. Does your spouse also have a health plan? What are the costs of being on his/her plan? Do a financial comparison to see if it's more cost-effective to be on your plan, factoring in the pre-tax benefit of paying higher payroll deductions by having a family plan.

Contribute towards a Health Savings Account

In 2025, the IRS permits you to contribute up to $4,300 if single coverage, or $8.550 if family plan, towards your health savings account. If age 55 or older at the end of the 2025 tax year, you can contribute an additional $1,000.[1] These totals must also include any employer contributions. Contributing these amounts via pre-tax will lower your taxable wages and also provide a higher net pay.

Health Savings Accounts are bank accounts combined with a high deductible medical plan which has a higher deductible than a traditional insurance plan. The IRS defines a high deductible health plan in 2025 as any plan with a deductible of at least $1,650 for an individual or $3,300 for a family.[1.]

Usually the monthly premium is lower, but you have to pay more health care costs yourself (your deductible) before the insurance company starts to pay its share. This allows you to pay for certain medical expenses with untaxed dollars that you contribute directly into the health savings account. Some employers also choose to make contributions to health savings accounts.

Read more about Health Savings Accounts in a later chapter of this book.

Contribute towards a Flexible Spending Account

Healthcare Flexible Spending Accounts are plans that allow you to deduct money from your paycheck on a pre-tax basis to cover unreimbursed and eligible health care expenses (as per the IRS). You can also set aside pre-tax money to pay for childcare and elder care services. The pre-tax money goes into an account managed by an FSA vendor.

Because the money that goes into your **FSA** is deducted from your income on a pretax basis, it lowers the amount of income on which you are taxed. For example, if you elected $1,400 annual FSA goal and you're in a 27% tax bracket, you could take home an extra $378 in a given year. S earch for FSA Tax Calculator on the internet to do your own estimates.

Understand the "Use It or Lose It" rules

Each Flexible Spending Account maintains guidelines and rules on how they administer the plan. Specifically, plan rules dictate what happens to unused money left in an account at the end of a plan year. Typically, there's a rollover feature which automatically rolls health care FSA money over into the next year.

Employers can choose from one of two rollover options: FSA with Grace Period and FSA with Carryover.

FSA with Grace Period
Allows any unused funds in a Health Care Flexible Spending Account at the end of a plan year to be available for 2 ½ months into the next plan year. Then, after the 2 ½ months, all unused funds are forfeited. You would essentially be able to reimburse yourself for eligible expenses incurred during that 2 ½ month period with any left-over funds from the prior plan year. You may be electing to contribute funds again in that next calendar year, so before those new funds are reimbursed, the FSA plan will use what's left over from the prior year first during the 2 ½ month window.

The filing deadline for claims is typically April 15 for submission of prior year claims.

FSA with Carry-over
Allows up to a certain amount of unused funds in a Health Care Flexible Spending Account to rollover into the next year and

continue to be available indefinitely as long as the employee is an active employee (or elects FSA with COBRA). You can still submit claims for reimbursement on prior year expenses which would reduce the carryover amount first before tapping into any new plan year contributions. For plans in 2024, the IRS allows a plan to permit up to $660 to be carried over into 2025, but this amount must be adopted by the plan.[2]

The Carry-over feature takes away the uncertainty of electing a Health Care Flexible Spending Account as most people don't like the idea of losing their money. The claim's filing deadline is typically March 31 for submission of prior year claims.

Any Healthcare FSA balances are forfeited when the employee leaves the company unless COBRA is elected. If they do not elect COBRA, then expenses can only be submitted up to the termination date. Therefore, if you leave your employer and have funds remaining in your Healthcare FSA, it's recommended you at least elect COBRA to continue your FSA. Then you'll have access to reimburse yourself for any out-of-pocket eligible healthcare expenses incurred after your termination date.

How do you know which FSA plan rules to follow?
There are several ways to find out. First is to contact the FSA vendor directly. They can answer this over the phone. Next, you can log online into your FSA account and then navigate to the plan rules. Look for a Frequently Asked Questions section.

A third way is to obtain a copy of the employer's SPD or Summary Plan Description of the FSA plan. By law, an employer is supposed to create and provide SPDs for cafeteria plans. I highly recommend you obtain a copy as the SPD goes into detail on how the FSA plan operates.

Dependent Care Flexible Spending Accounts don't have a rollover option. Unused money in that account is forfeited back to the plan. You may still have until March 31 or April 15, for example, to submit claims for that prior year money. My recommendation is to project, as accurately as possible, how much in childcare services you need to save for in the upcoming calendar year. Note that summer camps are eligible for reimbursement.

Pay for vision care services with your Health Savings Account

Instead of enrolling in a vision plan, use the money in your Health Savings Account to cover vision care expenses. Take what you would have contributed toward the payroll and make it a contribution to the HSA, and also increase your contribution to that HSA. That way you end up paying for things like eyeglasses, frames, and contact lenses with pre- tax dollars from your HSA. You would still have out of pocket expenses to pay for the eyewear as those plans never pay 100% of the charges; you always pay something. Why use post-tax money to pay for the eyeglasses or deplete a savings account?

Deductibles reset every plan year

It's a common experience: you finally have enough medical claims to reach your deductible level, but it's December and your doctor is scheduling that MRI or special test in January or February. Starting in January you have to start to meet your deductible all over again.
Very frustrating. It's important to plan in advance for having to meet your deductible all over again.
Try to schedule important medical visits and tests before the end of the plan year.

Get your preventive visits—they're covered at 100%

While many health plans included preventative services and covered them at 100% when obtained In-Network, it was not the standard for all insurance plans to cover until the Affordable Care Act was passed. ACA also defined a comprehensive set of preventive services that all adults, including women and children should have on a periodic basis.

Preventive care is widely held to be a significant strategy to manage and control one's physical health. Testing periodically for certain conditions, symptoms and health metrics aims to identify health risks and issues before they become a health problem and require higher level of medical care associated with increased costs.

A specific number of preventive services must be covered in all plans without your having to pay a copayment or co-insurance or meet your deductible. This applies only when these services are delivered by a network provider.

Read your benefits summary to learn more about what covered. You can also learn more by reading what the U.S. Preventive Service Task Force recommends, as well as what was passed under ACA.

https://www.uspreventiveservicestaskforce.org/

http://www.hhs.gov/healthcare/facts-and-features/factsheets/preventive-services-covered-under-aca/

Ask your doctor if the procedure being performed during that annual visit is actually considered preventive and covered by your insurance company. If they can't say yes for sure, ask why it's being performed?

You should be told in advance of why your doctor wants to perform a certain procedure. You should be informed of the value of a treatment or procedure that your doctor wants to perform on you and given the chance to say yes or no based upon medical evidence. How will this treatment or procedure help me, what are the risks, what will the outcome be?

You should be aware of the potential cost. If the doctor is Out- of-Network, your insurance radar should be on high alert as you'll be responsible for the cost regardless of whether it's covered by insurance.

If you're not comfortable with having a procedure done or are not 100% certain as to why it needs to be done, you have the option to postpone things. Reschedule until you can fully research, possibly obtain a second opinion.

Save Money Researching the Cost of Healthcare

If you have the time, researching the cost of a healthcare procedure before your appointment may save you money, or at the very least ensure you aren't surprised when you get the bill.

When dealing with a health condition, people can be consumed with their health as it may be a crisis or unexpected news. We're more concerned with the implications of a diagnosis on our health than what it may cost us. For some, it's the cost that will prevent them from taking the next step and getting the necessary treatment.
That's the time to pause and confirm what may be ahead of us financially. Having a clear picture of out-of-pocket costs can help to remove stress and allow you to focus on making the right decisions about our treatment.

Take radiology for example. The cost of an of x-ray can vary by provider. Health insurance plans negotiate the cost of procedures by provider in a given region further modifying the cost of a procedure. Many factors influence the negotiated price such as volume of care, clout and geographic area.

You may find if you're willing to do a little research, you could save yourself a few bucks. You may need to travel a few miles, but the cost difference may be worth it. Often, we're referred by our primary care doctor or specialist to a particular facility because they may be part of their network or practice. Don't feel obligated to go where your doctor says you should go if your research uncovers a better negotiated price at another facility. Let your doctor know your situation; they should be understanding.

Use the Cost of Care Search Tool Offered by Your Insurance Plan

Most health insurance companies provide a search tool on their website allowing you to search for the cost of care for a particular procedure, and also give you a listing of providers in your zip code area who offer that procedure along with the cost. It's essential that you ask your doctor for the full description and CPT Code of the procedure. The search tools require you be specific in your search. Otherwise, you may get incorrect results.

When you find the cost estimate from the online search tool, it typically applies the negotiated rate and any plan design features including whether you've met your deductible, giving you an estimated out-of-pocket cost for the procedure. If getting that test or procedure at another facility can save you money, go back to your doctor and ask them to give you the referral to that new facility. Your doctor will still get the results of the test sent back to them.

Use your EOBs to search for Previous Health Costs

If you're planning to get a test or procedure you received in the past, check out how much it cost. The EOB, or Explanation of Benefits, is the statement created when a claim is processed by your insurance plan. Log into your account on the insurance plan to search for old EOBs. If more than a year or two ago, the cost could go up due to inflation or other factors, but at least it can give you a ballpark to estimate the potential cost if performed by the same provider.

Price Transparency Tools

Over the past few years, efforts to increase price transparency to patients has yielded new sources of information the cost of care. While your insurance plan will provide the most accurate estimate on cost of care, there are other sources which can offer estimates which are not necessarily based on your specific health plan but will offer an average cost of care.

Fair Health provides tools to estimate the cost of care based on claims for medical and dental services paid for by private insurance plans, including the country's largest insurers.

Clear Health Costs is a journalism company from New York City bringing transparency to the health care marketplace by telling people what stuff costs using shoe-leather journalism, data journalism, investigative reporting and crowdsourcing.

Guroo.com was created by the Health Care Cost Institute (HCCI), an independent, nonprofit research organization. Guroo is powered by claims data contributed by some of the nation's key health insurance providers.

GoodRx helps you search for drug prices at different pharmacies and provides coupons. Insurance is often not used in conjunction with GoodRx.

Blink Health and BlinkRx offers discounted prescription prices on medications and can analyze your insurance, copay, and deductible to find your lowest prescription price.

Review and Compare

At the end of the day, you are in the driver's seat of your health care. Being health insurance literate means understanding your choices, finding the right care and knowing what your costs will be. Ask the doctor's office what the potential cost may be. They should be able to provide that, especially if they are In-Network with your insurance. You can always call your insurance plan for insights on costs.

Use coordination of benefits to your advantage

Are you and/or your family covered in more than one health plan or have the ability to be covered in more than one plan?

Based upon your circumstances, it may be beneficial to enroll in two different employer-based plans. Who would want to pay two sets of payroll contributions if one plan is perfectly fine to have? Well, if you have more than one health plan option available to you, and any of the following fit your situation, you may want to consider enrolling in both plans:

- o You plan to have significant health claims in the plan year.
- o Cost of being in one of the health plans is either free or ridiculously cheap.
- o The incremental cost of adding children is zero (you may already have the family plan which covers them).
- o One of the plans is a high deductible plan.
- o You're actively at work, covered in my employer's plan

and also over 65 enrolled in Medicare Part A/B/D or a Medicare HMO plan

o Your child or children will need orthodontia work (often, dental plans will cap the amount of orthodontia benefit paid out on an annual basis)

Coordination of benefits is an industry concept where health insurance companies follow a set of rules to determine which plan will pay first and which will pay second. Once the primary insurance pays, you can then submit the claim along with proof of what the primary insurance paid to that secondary health insurance carrier.

Typically, the employee's employer plan will be primary for them, and then any other plan would be secondary for them. Children, however, may follow the birthday rule: the plan of the parent whose birthday falls earlier in the year than the other parent will be the primary plan.

Basically, do the math. Does it make financial sense to contribute to both health plans through payroll contributions? What benefit would you essentially get out of both plans, and would it be more than the cost of contributing?

Elect COBRA if and when you need it

The Consolidated Omnibus Budget Reconciliation Act (COBRA) gives workers and their families who lose their health benefits the right to choose to continue group health benefits provided by their group health plan for limited periods of time under certain circumstances such as voluntary or involuntary job loss, reduction in the hours worked, transition between jobs, death, divorce, and other life events.

Qualified individuals may be required to pay the entire premium for coverage up to 102 % of the cost to the plan. The cost of the plan refers to what the full plan premiums may be, not necessarily the amount you were contributing through payroll deductions as an active employee.

If you are entitled to elect COBRA coverage, you must be given an election period of at least 60 days (starting on the later of the date you are furnished the election notice or the date you would lose coverage) to choose whether or not to elect continuation coverage. Once you elect and make your initial premium payment, your health coverage is reinstated back to the last date you were covered by the active employer plan. Therefore, you will not have a gap in coverage.

Losing your active health plan coverage from an employer plan without having another plan to replace it can be a frustrating and anxious time. In many cases, the loss of health coverage may also result in a time when our income is stopped. Therefore, it's understandable that we want to quickly enroll in a health plan. Keep in mind you have up to 60 days to make your election in COBRA. Therefore, you can postpone your election if you are planning to secure new employment which offers health insurance, and only elect and pay for COBRA if medical need is required.

How long can COBRA continue for?
COBRA requires that continuation coverage extend from the date of the qualifying event for a limited period of 18 or 36 months. When the qualifying event is the covered employee's termination of employment or reduction in hours of employment, qualified beneficiaries are entitled to 18 months of continuation coverage.

There are two conditions which could extend the period of COBRA beyond 18 months.

Disability - If any one of the qualified beneficiaries in your family is disabled and meets certain requirements, all of the qualified beneficiaries receiving continuation coverage due to a single qualifying event are entitled to an 11-month extension of the maximum period of continuation coverage (for a total maximum period of 29 months of continuation coverage). The plan can charge qualified beneficiaries an increased premium, up to 150% of the cost of coverage, during the 11-month disability extension.

Second Qualifying Event - If you are receiving an 18-month maximum period of continuation coverage, you may become entitled to an 18-month extension (giving a total maximum period of 36 months of continuation coverage) if you experience a second qualifying event that is the death of a covered employee, the divorce or legal separation of a covered employee and spouse, a covered employee's becoming entitled to Medicare (in certain circumstances), or a loss of dependent child status under the plan.

To learn more visit the Department of Labor website for COBRA: https://www.dol.gov/general/topic/health-plans/cobra

Are you eligible for Medicare and deciding whether to elect COBRA, too?

The rules for enrolling in COBRA may be complicated if you are eligible or enrolled in Medicare. I highly recommend you seek counsel from Medicare experts before making any decisions. This author is not an expert in Medicare or COBRA but knows enough that your choices may have negative consequences.

For example, if you are age 65 when you become eligible for COBRA (such as in the case of leaving an employer or losing eligibility for employer benefits), you are eligible to elect

COBRA at your qualifying event date. However, if you elect COBRA prior to turning age 65 but turn age 65 while on COBRA, you may lose your COBRA coverage for medical altogether. You will need to actively enroll in Medicare A/B/D or a Medicare HMO plan which goes into effect on your 65th birthday to ensure medical coverage is intact.

Beware: insurance companies will assume you've elected Medicare Part A and B if you also elect COBRA if age 65 or over. As a result, your medical claims will be paid as secondary by the COBRA medical plan. Insurance will assume Medicare is paying first. Therefore, consider whether paying the COBRA premiums and the Medicare monthly premiums at the same time are needed.

You may still need to elect COBRA for your spouse or children who are not Medicare-eligible. That's okay. COBRA allows you to continue medical coverage for eligible dependents only.

Medicare does not cover dental and vision services, so electing COBRA for dental and vision for yourself may make sense.

Use your Health Savings Account funds to pay for COBRA Premiums

Not widely known, accrued and unused money sitting your health savings account can be used to pay for your COBRA premiums. You may not be able to continue contributing into the health savings account after you've terminated your active medical plan, but you don't lose that money.

Use the telemedicine option through your medical plan

Telemedicine is the delivery of health care services using technology to connect over the phone, online video, or through secure e-mail for the evaluation and treatment of a healthcare condition. The service connects you with primary care doctors and health care practitioners who can treat you for a wide range of non-urgent medical conditions. Allergies, flu and cold, fever, rashes, sinus infections, and any number of other non-urgent medical conditions are some of the typical examples. Mental health is also a growing segment of the telemedicine market.

As of 2022, 90% of all firms with 50 or more employees and who offer health benefits cover telemedicine, a significant increase from 31% back in 2015.[3]

The increase in working-from-home and social distancing practices has increased awareness of telemedicine. Even before the onset of COVID-19, over 60% of health insurance plans, health institutions and hospital systems were offering telehealth as a viable, cost-effective and convenient option to treat patients for non-urgent medical issues.

A recent survey by the National Business Group on Health (NBGH) estimates that virtually all large employers (97 percent) make telehealth services available in states where it is allowed for acute care. Telehealth, and mental well-being will be offered by nearly all employers by 2026.[4.] Access is to a virtual medical provider is convenient. Providers are available 24/7, including after hours, nights, weekends and even holidays. You can typically access one within 30 minutes for a wide range of non-urgent conditions, and they are able to prescribe medications. The cost of a telemedicine visit can be less expensive than an actual in-office visit.

A recent study in the Journal of American Medical Association found that the average time for an in-office medical visit is 121 minutes, including time for travel, waiting, paying and completing paperwork. Within these two hours, only 20 minutes is actually spent face-to- face with the doctor. The entire encounter costs patients $43 in lost productivity.[5] The global telehealth market expects to grow to $15 billion by the end of 2028.[6.] Regardless of these statistics, telemedicine continues to have low utilization rates mainly because of barriers.

Quality of Physician
The practitioner using telemedicine technologies must be licensed to practice medicine in the jurisdiction where the patient receives treatment as dictated by current law. Generally, telemedicine providers require practitioners be board-certified which raises the level of quality.

Apprehensive may still exist if you're used to seeing your own doctor. Telemedicine providers, who maintain private practices, are professionally trained just like your own doctor to evaluate and treat patients. Telemedicine providers are experienced in handling telemedicine; they can quickly develop rapport and engage in the medical evaluation. At the end of the day, it's up to you whether to implement their treatment recommendation.

Conditions Treated
Telemedicine can support the evaluation and treatment of a wide range of non-urgent medical issues including:

Allergies Bronchitis
Cold, flu, cough
Constipation and Diarrhea Earache
Fever Headache

Insect bites
Pink eye
Respiratory
Sinus
Skin and rash problems
Mental health

If the medical condition is not something they can treat, they will provide recommendation for follow up with your own provider or referral to an emergency room if urgent/life threatening.

A number of telehealth providers offer specialty services to treat chronic conditions, as well as behavioral health.

Are you used to seeing doctor in the office?
The in-office experience often includes a series of steps such as check-in with the front office, interview by the nurse including check of your vitals, and then an interaction/meeting with the actual doctor.

The telemedicine process has similar steps, but instead you're going through the process virtually.

Essentially, the doctor will first have a conversation with you about your situation to understand and evaluate. If needed, they will ask for visual confirmation of the body part with the medical issue.
This can be done either by uploading a photo or sharing via two-way video chat through your mobile device or PC.

A telemedicine visit can be seen as a low-cost way to triage your situation starting small before embarking upon more time intensive, costly medical appointments that require in-person visits.

IT/Technology limitations
Mobile devices are ubiquitous. While you can access telemedicine through your computer, you have the option to download the telemedicine App to your mobile device utilizing all of the same features and tools as the web browser access. Therefore, access to telemedicine is limited by your own access to the internet or mobile service.

Laws are also in place to protect privacy. The HIPAA Privacy Rule is designed to be a minimum level of protection. Some states have even stricter laws in place to protect your personal health information. Telemedicine providers can share your information with your primary care physician in accordance with applicable state and federal laws.

Other Concerns
Underutilization of telehealth is widely attributed to a gap in benefit literacy or a lack of awareness. People also express an apprehension to use a credit card when paying for telehealth services.

Keep in mind that the cost of a telemedicine visit through your regular doctor may cost the same as if you were to visit your doctor in their office. Telemedicine providers like Teladoc, MDLIVE and AmWell offer access 24/7 operate differently, and may charge significantly less than what your regular doctor would charge.

Ask your health insurance company or your employer whether telemedicine is available.

Medical offices, like where your regular doctor practices medicine, may provide access to virtual medical visits, which may include access to your own primary care doctor or others within the same practice. MyChart, an online health connection for patients, provides the technology platform for face-to-face video sessions with doctors.

Check with your medical provider to see if they offer MyChart. Keep in mind the cost of a telemedicine visit through your regular doctor may cost the same as if you were to visit them in person for an office visit. Ask up front what the cost of the visit may be to avoid surprises later.

Telemedicine is here to stay. Access to healthcare is important. Learning how to use telemedicine can be a viable, cost-effective alternative to support our healthcare needs. To learn more about the telehealth industry, visit the **American Telehealth Association** website.

If you can get past the barriers, Telemedicine is a win/win as it allows you the flexibility to access medical treatment when needed. Also, it can minimize the amount of time to take time off from work having an effect on productivity.

Employees who use telemedicine use the service on weekends and holidays one third of the time. Telemedicine services are now expanding to support treatment for mental health, eldercare and even dermatology

Key Things to Do for a Successful Telemedicine Visit

Prepare in advance to use the service. Don't want until you need it to figure it all out. The service requires that you register all family members in advance, usually online.

Register payment information in your online account. You can use your Health Savings Account number or credit card.

Verify how the claim will be processed by your insurance. Do you have to submit a claim for reimbursement, or will the telemedicine vendor automatically bill the insurance company, then bill you in turn once your insurance processes the claim?

Keep the phone number and website information handy at all times. Put a copy in your wallet or on your mobile device. There may be an app to download.

Ask your employer or medical plan if they offer a telemedicine product. Teladoc, MDLIVE and AmWell are several of the more popular telemedicine providers. If telemedicine is not offered through your medical plan, you could also setup an arrangement directly with a telemedicine resource to gain access to this flexible and low-cost method of medical treatment.

Get Free Mental Health Services through the Employer Assistance Program

Employee Assistance Programs (EAP) are a free benefit offered to employees and household family members. EAPs provide confidential, professional services for a variety of personal and work- related issues. Probably one of the most undervalued programs offered, EAPs can serve as a personal concierge or referral service when you need help figuring things out.

EAPs have traditionally been known to offer crisis counseling or critical intervention quickly. Employees can access EAP on the telephone or online 24 hours a day, seven days a week. If you're having a stressful interaction with a co-worker, challenges raising your kids, or recently grieving a loss of a loved one, EAPs can do immediate intervention on the phone to help you manage through a crisis and can also refer you to a local mental health professional for face-to-face visits.

Most EAPs include three to five free face-to-face visits, some include more. This is a great way to seek mental health care on an outpatient basis for free. After the allotment of free visits, you can continue using the medical plan benefits coverage or not.

Look for the EAP resource in your company's benefits information.

Insider Tip: EAPs are often included as part of the Life and Disability insurance program, usually as an add-on feature for the employer. Contact the insurance company directly and ask them for the name and contact information of their EAP. You can also contact your employer or group administrator contact to research this for you.

Year End Health Plan Checklist to Avoid Costly Decisions

Before you head into a new calendar year, take inventory and prepare yourself for the unexpected with your health insurance plan. Here are a few items to consider:

- Is your health plan changing?

- Remember, deductibles and out-of-pocket credits don't rollover

- Did you get your preventive care check-up this year?

- Spend your FSA plan balance or risk losing it

While the majority of health plans renew on January 1, a small number of employer plans renew mid-year like July 1. These points can be applied when your plans' renewal comes up.

Is your health plan changing as of January 1?

Whether your insurance company is changing (moving from say Aetna to Cigna) or you elected a new health plan through the same insurance company, pay attention to slight variations that may impact you personally.

Changing your health plan could mean a change in the In-Network providers. Is your doctor still in the plan? If you have out-of- network coverage with your plan, you can continue to see your doctor if they are no longer in-network, but you will now be required to pay higher out-of-pocket costs. What if you have a medical procedure scheduled for early next year or you frequent a specific laboratory for frequent blood work, will your procedures be covered as expected?

Prescription benefits can change even if your plan is remaining the same, especially the formulary drug list. A formulary drug list is a list of prescription drugs covered by a prescription drug plan. Lists are typically created as a means of negotiating better prices to due volume. You could have been taking one medication made by one manufacturer but come to find out that it's no longer on the formulary list. You may be forced to take a new drug made by a different manufacturer or pay a higher price to keep the prior one.

Specialty medications are becoming more prevalent and also cost more money. As a result, special procedures and firms are now managing the fulfillment of specialty drugs. You may not be able to just visit your local pharmacy to get a drug filled. Specialty medications are often triaged to a pharmacy team at your health plan to help you manage your condition. This requires planning to ensure drug supplies are delivered timely, and if necessary that healthcare professionals are in place to administer the drug in your home. Check to see if your health plan instituted a new specialty medication process.

Deductibles and maximum out-of-pocket credits earned during the year do not rollover

You may want to get that visit in now before December 31 especially if you've met your deductible and you only have to pay co-insurance. Come January 1, your deductible resets to zero and you'll have to pay out of pocket from dollar until you meet your deductible again.

Preventive Care is Covered Annually, Every 365 days

Whether it's your medical, dental or vision plan, many services including preventive care are covered annually. However, this does not mean if you get your physical on January 15 if your last annual physical was November 15 in the prior calendar year. Most plans require you wait 365 days before your next preventive care visit is covered at 100%. Otherwise, services will either be denied or covered like a sick visit (subject to deductible or not at 100%). In rare cases, your plan may cover preventive care on a true calendar year basis. Dental plans may cover check-ups in this manner.

Also, keep in mind that preventive care may be tied to your age. Most health plans must cover a set of preventive services — like shots and screening tests — at no cost to you when provided by a doctor or other provider in your plan. This includes plans available through the Health Insurance Marketplace®. You or your children may have crossed over into a new age bracket whereby preventive care tests may or may not be covered anymore. Recommend you read your health plan's Summary Plan Description or the Summary of Benefits & Coverage to learn more about what's covered. You can also visit the **Healthcare.gov** site to learn more about preventive care.

Flexible Spending Accounts: Use it or Lose It

Healthcare FSA plans typically have a rollover feature for unused balances at the end of the calendar year. If you have more than the rollover limit, ideal for you to spend the excess funds now or make sure to submit your receipts to reimbursement before the claims deadline. In 2024, the IRS will allow plans to carryover $660 into 2025[2], but that does not mean all plans are required to allow the limit. Check your plan for details. **Summary of Action Items**

- Read your health plan materials and communications now to learn what changes to expect in the new plan year.

- Visit your health plan online account to verify where you stand on your deductible and maximum out of pocket met YTD. Schedule visits before the end of the year.

- Check to see if your prescription drug will be covered by the new plan.

- Review your FSA account to identify balances and file claims timely. Visit the **FSA Store** if you need a way to spend down your FSA funds.

- Contact your Benefits team or health plan to ask questions.

Appealing Your Claim

In 2023, on average 19% of in-network claims were denied by insurers who covered people receiving their health insurance through Healthcare.gov. Over 73 million claims out of 392 million in-network claims processed for Healthcare.gov plans were denied.[1] The percentage of claims denied did vary by state. Alabama had the highest denial rate at 34%, with South Dakota the lowest at 6%.

Why are claims denied?
Knowing why claims are denied may help you understand how to avoid them being denied in the first place.

- Administrative reason – 18%
- Denied as an excluded or not covered services – 16%
- Enrollee benefit limit reached – 12%
- Denied for lack of referral or prior authorization – 9%
- Denied for medical necessity – 5%
- Member not covered – 5%
- All others – 35% (includes reasons not listed)

Consumers rarely appeal denied claims (fewer than 1% of denied claims were appealed in 2023). When they did, insurers uphold their original decision 56% of the time. Another way of looking at this is 44% of the time claims appeals are approved or overturn the original denial.[1]

What can you do if your claim was denied or not paid correctly by insurance?

When your health claim is not paid as expected, you have a number of options or alternatives to pursue to get answers, and potentially have your health claim paid correctly or with a better outcome than initially processed.

Compare how the claim was paid to known plan design features

Administrative errors account for a good share of claim mishaps. This could be because your doctor submitted the claim with the wrong codes, dates of service, or even diagnosis. You were expecting the claim to be paid at 100%, for example, because it was related to a preventive visit, but it was applied to your deductible. This may be the case with mammograms, PAP, and PSA Tests. These tests are typically covered at 100% In-Network as they are considered Preventive Care. However, what if your doctor submitted the claim with a diagnosis code instead of a preventive code?

Your doctor will need to re-submit the claim directly to the insurance company to get reprocessed. That's the easiest and most expeditious remedy.

However, what if the insurance company isn't paying the claim according to what the plan benefits summary or documents reflect?

The plan document may say one thing, but the insurance processes it completely differently. For example, what if your plan document says Durable Medical Equipment is covered at 90% after deductible, but it's paying at 50% after deductible. Not good, right?

This can be remedied by first calling your insurance company to investigate. The insurance company representative should be able to research your insurance plan design on the phone and determine if the claim was processed incorrectly. If not, they should then be able to escalate it up to a supervisor.

Another alternative you should take simultaneously is to contact your employer benefits department or insurance agent. Make them aware of the discrepancy. It's not uncommon for an insurance company's system to be out of sync with a plan design. Your employer may have upgraded or changed their plan design for the new plan year, and the insurance system wasn't updated accordingly. The employer contact or insurance agent can and should intervene on your behalf. Why? When there's smoke, there's fire.

You may not be the only one who was impacted by this administrative mishap. A report should be run to identify anyone else who was adversely impacted, and subsequently have their medical claims reprocessed after the plan design is updated correctly.

Insurance company appeals

I recommend calling your insurance company first to talk through the outcome of the claim in question. You may be surprised to find that the denial is an administrative one that can be resolved by having the doctor resubmit the claim with corrected or missing information. But if it's not related to an administrative mishap, there are potentially other reasons why the claim was not paid according to your expectations.

Calling your insurance company serves another purpose related to your long game. Insurance companies typically record conversations that members have with the insurance customer service representatives. You want to put them on notice and have someone go to the mat for you as evidence that you've attempted to get your issue resolved. Down the road, if you file a formal appeal, your recorded conversation may come in handy by someone else in the appeals department.

If your claim was not the victim of an administrative snafu, the claim could have been denied for medical reasons, such as not being covered in the plan. In this case, the insurance company may need information about the appropriateness and effectiveness of a particular treatment or drug or technology. While insurance companies attempt to stay current with the health care industry, they may not always be aware of any recent changes in the industry.

Keep in mind that insurance companies will only cover items that are medically necessary and stipulated as such in their plan documentation, such as the Benefit Summary and Summary Plan Description.

If talking with the insurance company does not work, and/or your benefits/insurance agent confirms that, in their mind, the insurance company paid the claim correctly and accordingly to the plan design, the next option is to *file a formal appeal with the insurance company*. All insurance companies must provide standard appeal process whereby you and your doctor can submit a request or petition of sorts to have your health claim re-evaluated. This process may include two subsequent levels of appeal, so that after the first appeal is made, you can submit a second one.

You are required to submit appeal requests within a certain time frame after your claim was denied, typically 180 days. If you choose to file an appeal, it is important that you follow the appeals instructions printed in the denial letter and act within the designated timeframes. If you don't file your appeal within these timeframes, you lose your rights to further review of the decision

A third option may be to file an appeal with an external third party, not associated with the insurance company. Many health plans incorporate this external appeal process as a way to offer additional layers of review when the situation is merited.

Process summary for handling denied claims

There are typically 2 levels (or chances) to appeal through your insurance plan; find instructions for appeals on the EOB:

Write a letter to health insurance company to reconsider why claim should be covered. Get support of your In-Network provider (medical reasons?)

If out-of-network, probably write on your own. Include relevant facts to dispute decision

Occasionally a third external appeal is available through an independent third party. Your insurance company can provide their contact information which may be included in your final denial letter

Last resort: Contact your State Insurance Department. Contact the U.S. Department of Labor if your plan is considered an ERISA plan

State insurance department appeals and complaints

Finally, if you exhaust the standard in-house and external third-party appeal processes offered by the insurance company, you could always reach out to your state insurance department. The majority of state insurance departments have incorporated Independent Review Organizations (IROs) not connected with the insurance company who can review your appeals. While you are required to complete a form and provide sufficient documented detail about your case, it will generate the attention of the insurance company to formally respond in writing to your specific case.

While most state insurance departments do not publish statistics on the number of insurance claim appeals and their decisions, statistics from two states who do publish such data suggest that the odds are in your favor if you do appeal through an external party.

The State of Connecticut projected between 30% and 40% of claim denials were overturned through their External Review Program over a three- year period between 2010 and 2013.

According to the California Department of Insurance, between the years of 2001 and 2013, 43% of independent medical reviews cases were overturned in favor of the patient.

Under the Affordable Care Act (ACA) people with pre-existing conditions can't be denied a health policy because of a preexisting condition. But insurers can deny medical care if they consider it to be medically unnecessary. Under the ACA, all patients have the right to appeal denials through an external review. Before ACA, this was not the case.

Locate state insurance resources for complaints

The National Association of Insurance Commissioners (NAIC) maintains an online resource to make it easy for you to locate the consumer complaint resource for your state insurance department. **https://eapps.naic.org/cis/fileComplaintMap.do**

Many insurance companies offer an online complaint form that automatically gets forwarded to the appropriate department for handling your complaint. A listing of insurance company contacts for complaints is available later in this book.

Self-Insured Health Plan Appeals

Self-insured plans have the legal and compliance oversight of the Employee Retirement Income Security Act of 1974 (ERISA), a federal law that sets minimum standards for most voluntarily established pension and health plans in private industry to provide protection for individuals in these plans.

ERISA requires plans to provide participants with plan information including important information about plan features and funding; it provides fiduciary responsibilities for those who manage and control plan assets; it requires plans to establish a grievance and appeals process for participants to get benefits from their plans; and it gives participants the right to sue for benefits and breaches of fiduciary duty.

The Summary Plan Description or SPD of your plan should include information on how to file a complaint or submit an external appeal with the Department of Labor.

Tips on filing your appeal or complaint

Any appeal should provide additional information, supporting documentation, medical notes, or clarification about your claim not previously presented to the insurance company. Do not expect an insurance company to go out of their way to determine that the claim should have been paid to your liking. Generally, the person reviewing your appeal is looking at the information they have on file from your doctor such as the CPT codes, procedure codes, dates of service, diagnosis and other medical information on file.

Insurance claim denials that may warrant an appeal can fall into any number of categories:

- Services are not deemed medically necessary
- Services are no longer needed in that health care setting or level of care
- The effectiveness of the health care services has not been proven
- Services are considered experimental/investigational for treatment of this condition • Services are not a covered benefit
- Services submitted are duplicative to a previously submitted claim
- Incomplete information was submitted to process the claim
- Identifying the exact reason for your claim denial will help in providing the specific information needed by your insurance company to consider processing the claim.

You should be aware that you have the right to ask your treating physician to provide new information that would be helpful to your external review. Information from your treating physician may include:

- o A letter indicating the medical reasons that the requested service should be approved
- o Treatment notes from your treating physician that provide information on the medical care provided to you to date
- o The results of any relevant tests or procedures related to the requested service
- o Your own personal narrative or the narrative of an authorized representative describing the need for the requested service
- o For experimental or investigational treatments, any current medical literature or studies documenting the medical efficacy of the requested services

The appeal process could also include a peer to peer or direct conversation with your treating provider and the health insurance company. Be sure to include contact information for how the insurance company can best reach the doctor, including address, phone number, fax and e-mail. Your doctor could certainly call your health insurance plan, as well, to initiate the conversation especially if your doctor is in-network.

Reading the SPD (Summary Plan Description) will also help you prepare your appeal response. The SPD outlines what's covered and what isn't. It's important to understand the standard rules an insurance company may be using to cover a specific treatment. If you don't provide anything to challenge the existing rules, the insurance company could continue to expose how the claim is not a covered benefit according to plan SPD definitions. Therefore, know what the prevailing standard is and show how your situation is outside of those parameters.

What if my doctor recommends a treatment that is not covered by insurance?

Ask your doctor why they are advising a treatment not covered by insurance. You should be working in close partnership with your medical provider and have clear visibility into your treatment plans. Have you exhausted all other covered treatments and now have to find alternative methods?

In some cases, treatments for conditions may fall out of the norm. Insurance companies may need to be informed as to your history of treatment and how you've gone through all of the standard practices and treatments, and now alternative methods are needed. In this case, your doctor needs to do further advocating on your behalf.

Often, insurance companies will post their clinical guidelines on their public website explaining the medical, dental, and pharmacy services they may or may not cover. Their decisions are based upon objective, credible sources such as scientific literature, guidelines, consensus statements, and expert opinions. Therefore, in developing your appeal, you and your treating provider should reference the clinical guidelines to further understand the insurance company's position on why something may not be covered and assist you in crafting your argument as to why a particular treatment should be covered in your situation.

Understand the Rules of Enrollment

Employer or group-based health plans usually are setup as a cafeteria plan. This means the plan can provide a special exception to general federal income tax rules applicable to an employee's income.

Cafeteria plans allow employees to enroll in benefits and pay using pretax dollars, typically as a payroll deduction or contribution. Cafeteria plans follow Section 125 of the Internal Revenue Code.

Cafeteria plans also enable employers to deduct the costs of the plans as a non-taxable expense. Therefore, both employees and employers gain a tax advantage through the cafeteria plan approach.

Cafeteria or Section 125 plan must satisfy a number of conditions. Regulations are clear that any failure to operate in accordance with the terms of the plan or requirements of Section 125 will disqualify the plan, and both parties will lose the tax benefits.

One of the more employee-centric conditions of Section 125 relates to how and when cafeteria plan benefit elections can be elected and changed. Many of these same rules are followed by Marketplace ACA plans.

These moments in time when health insurance plans will allow you to enroll or make a change to your insurance plan. Here are the most common:

- As a new hire or newly eligible
- During Annual Open Enrollment

- Qualifying Events like a birth, marriage, divorce or loss of eligibility such as workforce reduction, resignation or reduction in work hours impacting benefits eligibility

Each of these windows of opportunity have their own special rules governing what you can change, how long you have to make the change and what, if any, documentation is required to support the change.

Why have rules to determine when benefit elections can be made?

At the core of insurance is a sense of predictability. What do you think would happen to insurance premiums if employees were permitted to enroll in and out of insurance when they only needed it? There wouldn't be sufficient premiums collected to cover the risk.

The insurance underwriters make predictions or actuarial calculations to estimate what premiums to charge based upon the group census or demographics of a group, as well as how many people are enrolled in a plan. From this demographic data, they can predict their medical exposure or risk. The more risk, the higher premiums they want to charge to cover potential costs. Insurance companies want to make money—let's face it—they are a business. However, they also need to cover the projected medical costs.

Self-insured employers, on the other hand, are not trying to make money. Instead, they want to break even or at least cover their costs which include claims and administrative costs. Without having predictability in who will be enrolled, costs can be unexpected and unpredictable.

Fairness is another important factor that employees need to have institutionalized in the process. Employees need a sense of fairness or empowerment, otherwise, decisions would be made without any rhyme or reason.

If you want to learn more about cafeteria plans, you can google Section 125. However, you should also be able to read your employer's cafeteria plan document. Ask your benefits contact for a copy. A version may also be posted for all employees to see on the employer's intranet. Either way, employers or health plans through Healthcare.gov are supposed to make plan compliance documentation required by law available to employees on a timely basis.

New Hire / Newly Eligible Rules

As a newly eligible, you typically get up to 30 days to submit benefit elections. Therefore, if you don't submit your benefit elections on time, you will go without insurance benefits until one of the next eligible windows.

A growing trend with employers is to offer an automatic enrollment feature in their cafeteria plans. One common practice is to automatically enroll new hire employees into a default medical plan, usually the lowest cost plan for employee-only coverage, if you don't make an active election within your newly eligible period. Automatic Enrollment features make it required for you to opt out of medical coverage. Thereafter, elections can continue to be evergreen meaning they continue from year to year unless you make an active election during an open enrollment period. (More on open enrollment shortly).

Employers are required to provide sufficient and adequate communication about the automatic enrollment feature at the time of hire and before the beginning of each plan year. Employers may also call this feature an automatic rollover during the open enrollment period; if you don't make an active election during that period, your same benefits will rollover into the next plan year.
More on open enrollment later in this section.

The new hire period is usually a good time to make other benefit elections, such as in life insurance or disability benefits, which may be paid on a post-tax basis and not part of the cafeteria plan.

Insurance companies offer a guaranteed issue amount without requiring you to answer medical questionnaire or complete a physical. Often, a guaranteed amount of life insurance is offered, no questions asked. If you ask to elect life insurance after your new hire period, the insurance company will require proof of good health status as they may think you're only enrolling later/down the road because you need it (have a life situation such as an illness, operation or other risk situation occurring now or in the near future).

Associate-paid life insurance is usually paid using after tax payroll contributions. As a result, you should be able to make changes to your life insurance elections at any time (increase, decrease benefit amounts). However, your employer or life insurance plan may provide different rules for when you can make such changes.

Therefore, the new hire and open enrollment periods are probably one of the most crucial times to submit your elections as it will set the tone for the rest of the calendar year.

Life Events (changing benefits mid-year)

There a numerous life events when you may need to make changes to your health benefits. Health plans are designed to support enrollment changes when such life event changes, but you need to know the rules of engagement.

What are examples of life events?

- Getting married
- Domestic partnership
- Having a baby, adoption
- Getting divorced
- Children turning 26 or other age and no longer eligible for benefits
- Spouse's employer offers open enrollment at a different time of the year than yours
- Changing jobs, a new job, or a promotion with a large salary increase
- You or your spouse lose eligibility through employer
- You go on disability or take a health leave of absence (Family Medical Leave) either for yourself or a family member
- Moving across the country or out of an insurance plan's service area
- Medicare eligibility

While not exhaustive, you get the idea. Your employer or health plan, though, will require you to provide documentation to support the change. For example, a marriage certificate, birth certificate, or letter from other employer or insurance company. These documents should include the date last covered, names of family members impacted, and be printed on letterhead of an official entity like the insurance company or other employer.

Submit the letter and benefit election change within the required time frame, usually 30 or 31 days. I recommend that you not only email the letter to appropriate contact at your employer, but also follow up with a call. Make sure you get a live response to confirm receipt and that they accept the election and documentation change. You need proof of confirmation.

Your employer is supposed to publish rules for making life event benefit changes. This may be a separate document posted on their intranet or maintained within another insurance plan document. Employers that are self-insured are required to maintain and make available to employees ERISA plan document which will include general language on life event changes called the **Group Health Plan Summary Plan Description (SPD)**. Ask your employer for this reference. If the employer is fully-insured, the insurance company provides a general Summary Plan Description which outlines rules and procedures for making benefit changes.

Employers are required to share compliance documents with employees, either by mailing them or making available to an intranet. Check your company's website for such documents. If they are not posted, request them directly through Human Resources or Benefits Department. Your request for a compliance document needs to be fulfilled within 30 days by law.

You can google the phrase "qualified life events" and you'll find dozens of links to documents posted by employers, vendors and government agencies, but be careful as their documents may be out of date and not specific to your employer plan.

Insider Tip: Life event rules are considered guidelines with flexibility in employer discretion. Exceptions to the rule may happen. For example, say you forgot to add your newborn within 31 days of the date of birth. You can contact your employer or health plan to explain the situation. Rather than wait until the next open enrollment, they may be able to approve enrollment immediately and not retroactively back to the date of birth. At least you can have coverage for the rest of the calendar year. This is often more common with employer groups who are self-insured and not fully-insured. Employers who make exceptions try to do so in a consistent manner. ACA plans may be more restrictive and not permit changes outside of the normal 31-day window unless there are extenuating circumstances.

Annual Open Enrollment

The time of the year when health plan participants can make benefit plan changes, usually lasts up to several weeks or longer, and is completed before the new plan year starts. Most benefit plan years runs from January 1 through December 31, so the open enrollment period could run from October to November. However, some employers offer a mid-year plan which may start in April or June, for example. This is often done for business reasons to balance resources within an organization. Conducting benefits open enrollment during the 4th quarter may interfere with the busiest time of the year for an organization. As a result, the open enrollment period could run in February through May.

Employers will communicate in advance of the annual open enrollment period informing employees about plan options, costs, and how to make your election changes. Enrollment is done online, by paper, or in-person. Technically, as long as the new plan year election is received prior to the beginning of the new plan year, an employer can accept benefit plan election changes. You may need to formally request a change if the enrollment period is over.

The open enrollment period is a self-imposed period of time to ensure an employer has sufficient time to receive, audit and send benefit election changes to insurance vendors who then need time to process all of the customer requests, produce new ID cards and prepare enrollments for the next plan year.

Insider Tip: During open enrollment, you can typically make a lot of plan changes without providing documentation to justify a change as in the case of a mid-year life event. This includes adding or removing dependents, dropping or adding new coverage, increasing or lowering contributions to health savings, flexible spending accounts.

Remember, if you failed to submit a mid-year life event benefit change within the required timeframe (31 days for example), the annual open enrollment period is the time to make any necessary changes.

The Health Insurance Marketplace available through HealthCare.gov generally follows the same timeline for enrolling or making changes during their Open Enrollment period:

- **November 1:** Open Enrollment starts — first day you can enroll in, renew, or change health plans through the Marketplace for the coming year. Coverage can start as soon as January 1.
- **December 15:** Last day to enroll in or change plans for coverage to start January 1.
- **January 1:** Coverage starts for those who enroll in or change plans by December 15 and pay their first premium.
- **January 15:** Open Enrollment ends — last day to enroll in or change Marketplace health plans for the year. After this date, you can enroll in or change plans only if you qualify for a Special Enrollment Period.
- **February 1:** Coverage starts for those who enroll in or change plans December 16 through January 15 and pay their first premium.

Mid-Year election events

Section 125 cafeteria plans generally do not permit changes to pretax elections during the plan year or period of coverage. This is known as the irrevocability of elections. However, exceptions to the rule exist, and they are typically known as life events or situations that occur in life enabling you to make election changes mainly because your life situation results in an opportunity to reevaluate your benefit elections and enroll in plans that make more sense supporting your life.

If a benefit is elected on a post-tax basis (usually life insurance or disability coverage), you may be able to change these elections at any time throughout the plan year subject to your employer's benefit enrollment process.

The following chart illustrates a number of the most common exceptions to the irrevocability rule, enabling you to change your pre- tax benefits mid-year. This list is not intended to be a complete and comprehensive list. Please refer to your employer or plan administrator's plan rules for guidelines and rules that support making mid-year election changes. You can also do a search on the Web using the term "mid-year benefit election rules" and find any number of resources on this topic.

Typically, mid-year benefit election requests need to be submitted to the employer or benefits administrator within 30 days of the life event date along with supporting documentation documenting the life event.

The Affordable Care Act allows application for health insurance during a Special Enrollment Period (SEP) if you experience a qualifying life event including: losing health coverage, moving, getting married, having a child.

Mid-Year Life Event	Description
Change in Employment Status	Commencement of employment, return from an unpaid leave of absence, or a change in worksite. Change from part-time to full-time or hourly to salaried. Termination is also a change in employment status. Can include Spouse and dependent children
Termination and Rehire within 30 days	An employee who is terminated but then rehired within 30 days of the termination will have prior elections reinstated and there is no opportunity for mid-year election change.
Termination and Rehire after 30 days	Regulations treat this change in status as a new hire and the employee may make new elections.
Marriage or newly eligible domestic partner	May enroll or increase election to include his or her new spouse, domestic partner and/or dependents; may also revoke or decrease elections only when the coverage becomes effective or is increased under the significant other's plan
Divorce, Legal Separation, Death of Spouse	The relationship of the covered spouse to the employee changes, or no longer is eligible for coverage in the plan based upon the definition of their relationship
Number of dependents change	Includes birth, adoption, placement for adoption, death of dependent, or becomes a new dependent through marriage or domestic partnership
Change in place of residence	If a residential move changes eligibility for a plan which is upon geographic factors, such as moving out of a network region or coverage area of a health plan.
Significant cost changes due to automatic increases or decreases in elective contributions	If the cost of a benefit plan changes during a period of coverage, the plan may allow employee to make an election change.

Loss of coverage	Employee is no longer eligible for coverage, such as reduction in hours, loss of employment, COBRA coverage is exhausted.
Loss or gain of eligibility for Medicaid or CHIP	Can elect (or drop) coverage for employee, spouse or dependent who has lost (or gains) Medicaid or CHIP coverage (Child Health Insurance Program)
Judgment, Decree or Order resulting in change in legal custody	When legal custody of a child changes and requires an employee to provide health coverage for that child. May cancel coverage is the order provides for another plan to cover the child or dependent.
Entitlement to Medicare or Medicaid	When an employee, spouse or dependent who is enrolled in the employer's health plan becomes entitled to Medicare or Medicaid, the employee may elect to cancel or reduce coverage. Loss of coverage in Medicare or Medicaid creates opportunity for employee, spouse or dependent to enroll in the employer health plan.
FMLA Leave of Absence	Employees can make election changes. If the employee is on an unpaid leave of absence, the employee may revoke coverage or continue coverage but discontinue payment of his or her share of the contribution during the leave. The employer can collect missed contributions upon return to work.
Return from FMLA leave	Employee returning from an FMLA leave may make a new election if his or her coverage terminated while he or she was on FMLA leave. The employer may reinstate the employee in his or her prior elections upon return from leave.

112

Privacy and HIPAA

When you walk into a doctor's office, are you ever handed a privacy notice and asked to sign a document verifying you received it?
Have you ever read the notice they give you? That's because health care provides, among other groups or entities, are required by law to obtain verification they informed you.

The Health Insurance Portability and Accountability Act of 1996 (HIPAA) is a federal law that sets rules about who can look at and receive your health information. This law gives you rights over your health information and when it can be shared. It also requires your doctors, pharmacists and other health care providers, and your health plan to explain your rights and how your health information can be used or shared. This requirement is done by sharing a copy of an official privacy Notice.

The U.S. Department of Health and Human Services recommends you follow four basic steps to make sure you understand the privacy Notice and your rights

- Get a copy of the Notice of Privacy Practices
- Read the Notice
- Ask questions about the Notice or Your Rights
- Know what you are signing

Most of us believe that our medical and other health information is private and should be protected, and we want to know who has this information. The Privacy Rule, a federal law, gives you rights over your health information and sets rules and limits on who can look at and receive your health information. The Privacy Rule applies to all forms of individuals' protected health information, whether electronic, written, or oral. The Security Rule is a federal law that requires security for health information in electronic form.

Entities that must follow the HIPAA regulations covered entities include:

Health Plans, including health insurance companies, HMOs, company health plans, and certain government programs that pay for health care, such as Medicare and Medicaid.

Most Health Care Providers—those that conduct certain business electronically, such as electronically billing your health insurance—including most doctors, clinics, hospitals, psychologists, chiropractors, nursing homes, pharmacies, and dentists.

Health Care Clearinghouses—entities that process nonstandard health information they receive from another entity into a standard (i.e., standard electronic format or data content), or vice versa.

What Information Is Protected

Information your doctors, nurses, and other health care providers put in your medical record.

Conversations your doctor has about your care or treatment with nurses and others.

Information about you in your health insurer's computer system.

Most other health information about you held by those who must follow these laws.

Why should I really care about HIPAA and my privacy?

For the most part, we probably don't have control over where or how our information is shared. In this day and age, so much information is shared electronically, which makes the business of health care go more efficiently. However, you probably want to know where your health information is going and why. Ask your doctor or health care provider how you can access your health record especially if stored electronically or online.

To learn more about HIPAA and your privacy rights as a consumer, visit the U.S. Department of Health and Human Services website at **https://www.hhs.gov/hipaa/for-individuals/guidance-materialsfor- consumers/**.

Health Savings Accounts

What is a Health Savings Account (HSA)?

As defined by the Internal Revenue Service, an HSA is a trust or a custodial account setup with a qualified HSA trustee to pay or reimburse certain medical expenses you incur. You must be an eligible individual to qualify for an HSA. Additionally, as long as you are enrolled in a High Deductible Health Plan (HDHP), you may open and contribute to an HSA.

In laymen's terms, an HSA is essentially a bank account to deposit money that you can use at a later time to pay for, reimburse or cover eligible out-of-pocket healthcare expenses (as defined by the IRS) for yourself or an eligible dependent. Out-of-pocket means expenses not reimbursed or paid by your insurance such as medical, dental or vision plan. The individual, not the employer, owns the HSA. You and/or your employer can make contributions into this account benefitting from a tax deduction.

Contributions made to the account are typically done on a pre-tax basis as a payroll deduction from your paycheck, excluded from gross income. This enables you to benefit from a lower taxable payroll base, where you may pay less in taxes and increasing your take-home pay. Contributions can be made directly into an HSA, and not as a payroll deduction. This method requires you to file this contribution on a future Federal Income Tax return in order to benefit from the tax deduction.

Watch-Out: If you make contributions into your HSA as a payroll deduction AND directly into your HSA via a non-payroll deduction method, make sure you do not contribute more than the annual calendar year limit allowed. Why? You will run into tax issues that will have to get addressed. Such "over" contributions would need to be removed from the account prior to the tax year filing date to avoid tax penalties.

The contributions into an HSA benefit from what's known as the Triple Tax Advantage:

Tax-deductible: You contribute through pre-tax payroll deductions, or you contribute outside of your payroll deductions and take the tax deduction on your income tax return.
Tax-free: Withdrawals to pay qualified expenses are never taxed. **Tax-deferred:** Interest earnings on investments are not taxed, and if used to pay qualified expenses, remain tax-free.

Additionally, all contributions into an HSA are yours to keep: Unlike a healthcare flexible spending account, unused money in your HSA isn't forfeited at the end of the year; it continued to grow, tax-free.

The rules and tax laws for Health Savings Accounts are quite long and complicated. The following summary of HSA's is intended to help summarize how they work and what they are about. Information was drawn in part from the **IRS Publication 969 Cat. No. 24216S Health Savings Accounts and Other Tax-Favored Health Plans**, as well as from other information provided publicly through various HSA administrators which can be found on the internet.

What can I use health savings account funds for?

The IRS determines which expenses are eligible for reimbursement. Eligible expenses include health plan deductibles, copayments or coinsurance, dental work and orthodontia, eyeglasses and contact lenses, and prescriptions which are covered by your plan, but were not reimbursed in their entirety. The IRS allows for reimbursement on a wide array of eligible expenses that are not normally covered by your health plan and are available over the counter at your local pharmacy.

Here's a short list of eligible items you can use your health savings account for:

> Acne Treatments (over the counter) with an Rx
> Bandages and related items
> BP monitor
> Hair treatments (with letter from your doctor)
> Hearing aids and batteries
> Pregnancy tests (over the counter)
> Sleep aids
> Transportation, parking and related travel expenses (essential to receive eligible care)
> Vitamins (prescription) with a letter from your doctor
> Weight loss program (for treatment of a medical condition)

Note: Items may require a prescription and/or letter from a doctor. Final determination would be made by the health savings account administrator. This list is intended to provide examples of eligible expenses and not serve as the final word on what is eligible.

Your HSA plan can provide detailed examples of what may be considered an eligible expense. You may also want to check out The HSA Store, an online and easy-to-understand educational resource for HSA-eligible products. Visit them on https://hsastore.com/HSA-Eligible-Items.aspx.

Who can use a health savings account?

To be an eligible individual and qualify for an HSA, you must meet the following requirements:

- You are covered under a high deductible health plan (HDHP) on the first day of the month.

- You have no other health coverage except what is permitted as other health coverage by the IRS, such as a limited purpose FSA.

- You are not enrolled in Medicare or Tricare.

- You cannot be claimed as a dependent on someone else's tax return.

The federal government does not recognize domestic partners as spouses. Unless a domestic partner qualifies as a dependent under the Internal Revenue Code, expenses on behalf of the domestic partner are not eligible for reimbursement from the Health Savings Account. Please reference the **IRS Publication 969** for additional rules on HSA eligibility.

How much can I contribute to a health savings account each year?

In calendar year 2025, the annual maximum contribution is $4,300 if you have a single coverage (self-only), and $8,550 if you cover one or more dependents on your high deductible health plan.

The maximum contribution limit must also take into account contributions made by your employer. The annual maximum contribution limit allowed by law that you can make is reduced by any contribution your employer provides into your

Health Savings Account. For example, if your employer contributes $500 into your HSA, your annual limit is reduced from $4,300 to $3,800 if you have self-only coverage

Additional Catch-Up contribution. If you are an HSA eligible individual who is age 55 or older at the end of your tax year, your contribution limit is increased by $1,000. This is known as the "catch-up contribution". For example, if you have self-only coverage, you can contribute up to $5,300 in 2025 (the contribution limit for self-only coverage ($4,300) plus the additional contribution of $1,000).

Also, what they mean by "or older at the end of your tax year", is if you turn age 55 at any point in the calendar year, you can make the full $1,000 catch-up contribution at any point in that same calendar year. You do not have to wait until you turn age 55 later in the year. The contribution can be made as a lump sum or divided up by the number of remaining pay periods

How do I use a health savings account or access the funds?

Since HSAs are essentially a bank account, accessing the funds is basically like how you would utilize money in a checking account. Withdrawing funds from an HSA is called a disbursement. **Debit Card.** HSAs issue a debit card which can be used pay for your out-of-pocket expenses (what you owe) like any other credit or debit card. Most health care professionals accept payment via credit or debit card.

The HSA debit card can be used at a retail pharmacy or mail- order prescription program through your insurance company. The HSA debit card can be setup with a PIN to access funds for withdrawal from an ATM machine. Find out if your HSA administrator charges fees for ATM withdrawals.

Word of advice: try not to pay the health care professional when you are leaving their office. Request they submit the claim first through your insurance plan. This will allow for any special claims processing discounts to apply, including any payments to be made by the insurance company. Once processed, the insurance company will indicate the Amount You Owe on the EOB or Explanation of Benefits Statement. Once you overpay a provider, it may be hard getting those funds back. Therefore, recommended you wait to pay.

Checks. HSAs provider can issue you a checkbook from which you make payments for eligible services. Fees are usually assessed for ordering checkbooks, so this may not be the most cost-effective method. Fees are deducted directly from your HSA.

An alternative method to pay healthcare providers is via check but issued online from your account itself. Unlike Electronic Funds Transfer, you can submit a request to pay a provider directly from the HSA. The provider would receive a check in the mail. This method typically does not carry an extra fee.

Electronic Funds Transfer. You can also transfer funds into your own personal account. You could pay for your out-of-pocket health care expenses using non-HSA monies from a credit card, check or cash. Then, later on you can reimburse yourself from the HSA. Be sure to retain receipts or copies of invoices to support the funds you withdrew.

Is there an impact on my income taxes using a health savings account?

Contributions into your HSA are typically made via payroll deductions on a pre-tax basis which lowers your overall gross income subject to Federal taxes. In most states, the same tax treatment applies. However, California and New Jersey are two states that do not offer tax-free contributions at the state level while all states are exempt from federal government taxes on HSA contributions.

As long as you use HSA funds for eligible health care expenses as defined by the IRS, you would fine from a tax perspective. If you use the funds for something other than an eligible expense, you will need to pay tax on the funds used, plus a penalty of 20%. For example, if you used $500, the penalty would be $100.

If an individual is over 65 and enrolled in Medicare, they are able to use the funds for non-qualified distributions (expenses that are not on the approved eligible IRS list). Taxes would be applied for these distributions, but a penalty would not. Please consult your tax advisor for further advice.

There are several tax forms issued by the health savings account administrator. These forms may be mailed out or available for download from your health savings account:

- IRS Form 1099-SA is provided for each HSA distribution you made in the current tax year.
- IRS Form 5498-SA indicates your HSA contributions made for the current tax year.

What if I am eligible for Medicare? (Age 65 or older) If you're still enrolled in a HDHP through your employer with a health savings account, and will turn age 65, you need to make a thoughtful decision. The IRS does not allow you to be enrolled in Medicare AND make or receive contributions into an active health savings account.

Medicare Part A covers hospitalization and Medicare Part B covers outpatient services. Drug coverage is available through Part D. Medicare HMOs cover all the services under Parts A, B and typically D.

The decision to elect Medicare is a separate and distinct process altogether. A number of factors come into play:

Will you be actively working after age 65 and still eligible for your employer health plan?
If yes, does it make sense to pay Medicare premiums each month for Part B when the Part B coverage will potentially be considered secondary coverage? Medicare Part B premiums can run upwards of $150 per month, or $1,800 annually. What kind of coverage would you need through Medicare Part B if your employer-based plan was paying as primary for most expenses? Medicare covers 80%. Your out-of-pocket expenses would consist of plan deductibles and coinsurance, along with payroll contributions.

You'd have compare the financial investment of Medicare Part B against what your out-of-pocket exposure would be with the employer plan.

Medicare Part A is typically considered an automatic enrollment upon age 65. As long as you've paid in your 10 years of Medicare payroll tax, you would be eligible to elect (or what I like to call enact) Medicare Part A for hospital coverage. Most people consider this a no-brainer because you don't have to pay Medicare Part A monthly premiums like you do with Medicare Part B. You receive a letter in the mail from CMS (Centers for Medicare Services) well in advance of your 65th birthday informing you of how to enact Medicare Part A and elect Medicare Part B.

However, here's the caveat: The IRS doesn't care if you're only enrolled in Medicare Part A; you cannot make or receive contributions into your health savings account if you enact Medicare Part A only, or both Parts A and B. **If you're still employed at age 65, seriously consider whether it's worthwhile to enact Medicare Part A as you would stop making and/or receiving contributions into your health savings account.**

This author is not a Medicare coverage expert but is able to share his experience managing employer plans and potential watchouts if Medicare is also involved. You should engage with Medicare expert to understand implications of your Medicare enrollment on your particular financial situation.

If you have the income to spare, continue to make contributions into your HSA as it's financially advantageous to do so. Saving for current or future medical expenses may be critical. Remember, you can also use HSA funds down the road to pay for your Medicare premiums, Long Term Care Premiums, and even COBRA premiums.

Hopefully, your employer offers more than one medical plan option (other than the HDHP). If you did elect to enroll in Medicare and continued to work after age 65, you would need to change your medical plan out of the HDHP into a non-HDHP plan to avoid any tax implications on the HSA contributions.

If your spouse is on your employer HDHP with HSA and is turning age 65, and you are under age 65, the IRS allows you to continue making and / or receiving contributions into your HSA while your spouse elects Medicare Part A, or A and B. He/she would be eligible to use the HSA funds as well to cover unreimbursed eligible HSA expenses as long as they are an eligible dependent.

If you are currently over age 65, enrolled in a HDHP with a HSA, and enrolled in Medicare, you may want to consider changing your medical plan as soon as possible. The IRS will most likely catch up to you through an income tax return. Consult a tax advisor for further advice, and even the advice of your HSA administrator.

You are allowed to contribute to your HSA in the year you turn 65 but must prorate the annual contribution limit for the number of months eligible for that year. The other option is to un-enroll from Medicare. See the advice from the Social Security Administration.

What's the difference between a health savings account (HSA) and a healthcare flexible spending account (FSA)?

In some respects, HSAs and FSAs are the same. Each are a viable way to use contributions made into a savings account on a tax preferred basis to reimburse yourself or pay for eligible health care expenses. FSAs were initially offered through employer-based plans in the 1970s whereas HSAs were introduced around 2004. There are more differences, though, than similarities.

Eligibility Requirements
You must be enrolled in a High Deductible Health Plan (HDHP) to contribute to a health savings account where a Healthcare FSA can be a stand-alone, independent plan.

Annual Contribution Limits
2025 contributions are capped at $4,300 for single coverage, $8,550 for family coverage; FSA contribution limit is $3,300.

Changing Contribution Limits
HSA plans can allow for frequent changes to your contribution levels throughout the plan year. FSA changes are only permitted during certain qualifying mid-year life events.

Eligible Expenses

The list of eligible expenses you can reimburse yourself from either plan is identical. However, if you elect an FSA while also enrolled in a medical plan with a HSA, your FSA funds can only be used for dental or vision expenses. The FSA becomes a limited-purpose plan.

Rollover of Funds

Any unused HSA funds at the end of the calendar year will rollover, and you never lose your funds. FSA plans have a "use it or lose it" provision where you forfeit unused funds, with some exceptions where a certain amount may be carried over to the next plan year.

Changing Employers

HSA funds follow you when you change employers; your funds remain yours to use on eligible expenses. You are permitted to have another / new HSA with a different health plan/bank. FSA plans stop when you leave your employer. You may be permitted to continue contributing to the FSA on COBRA but only for the rest of the current calendar year you leave your employer.

Taxes

For both plans, contributions are tax-deductible or made on a pretax basis from your payroll. Distributions for approved IRS expenses are tax-free.

Enrolled in Medicare

Cannot make contributions to HSA if also enrolled in Medicare. You can continue to make contributions to an FSA if enrolled in Medicare.

To learn more about the various programs designed to give individuals tax advantages to offset health care costs, read the IRS Publication 969 https://www.irs.gov/pub/irs-pdf/p969.pdf.

State Insurance Departments

Alabama Department of Insurance Consumer Services Division
P. O. Box 303351
Montgomery, AL 36130-3351
334-241-4141 Fax:
(334) 956-7932
http://www.aldoi.gov/consumers/FileComplaint.aspx

Alaska Department of Commerce, Community and Economic
Development
Division of Insurance
550 W. 7th Avenue, Suite 1560
Anchorage, AK 99501-3567
(907) 269-7900 insurance@alaska.gov
https://www.commerce.alaska.gov/web/ins/Consumers/FileaConsumerComplaint.aspx

Arizona Department of Insurance 100 North 15th Avenue, Suite 261
Phoenix, AZ 85007-2630
602-364-2499 consumers@azinsurance.gov
https://insurance.az.gov/consumers/help-problem/filing-complaint

Arkansas Insurance Department Consumer Services Division 1200
West Third Street
Little Rock, AR 72201-1904 800-852-5494 or
501-371-2640
insurance.consumers@arkansas.gov
http://www.insurance.arkansas.gov/csd-complaint.htm

California Consumer Assistance Program
Operated by the California Department of Managed Health Care and
Department of Insurance
980 9th Street, Suite 500
Sacramento, CA 95814
888-466-2219 800-927-4357
http://www.healthhelp.ca.gov http://www.insurance.ca.gov/01-
consumers/101-help/

Division of Insurance, Colorado Department of Regulatory Agencies
1560 Broadway, Suite 850
Denver, CO 80202
303-894-7490
800-930-3745
Dora_insurance@state.co.us
https://www.colorado.gov/pacific/dora/ask-question-make-
complaintdivision-insurance

Connecticut Office of the Healthcare Advocate
PO Box 1543
Hartford, CT 06144
866-466-4446. Consumer Affairs External Review Unit. 860-297-3910
Healthcare.advocate@ct.gov http://www.ct.gov/oha/site/default.asp

Delaware Department of Insurance Consumer Services Division
841 Silver Lake Blvd Dover, DE 19904
800-282-8611. 302-674-7310 Fax: 302-739-6278
consumer@state.de.us https://www.colorado.gov/pacific/dora/ask-
question-make- complaintdivision-insurance

Florida Department of Financial Services Division of Consumer Services
200 East Gaines Street
Tallahassee, FL 32399
Statewide Toll-Free: 877-693-5236 Out of State: 850-413-3089
TDD Line: 800-640-0886
Consumer.services@myfloridacfo.com
https://apps.fldfs.com/eService/Default.aspx

Georgia Office of Insurance and Fire Safety Commission Two Martin Luther King, Jr. Drive
West Tower, Suite 704 Atlanta, Georgia 30334
Main Telephone: 404-656-2070
Toll Free: 800-656-2298 Fax: 404-657-8542
https://www.oci.ga.gov/ConsumerService/complaintprocess.aspx

Hawaii Insurance Division Health Insurance Branch PO Box 3614
Honolulu, HI 96811
808-586-2804 Fax: 808-587-
5379
http://cca.hawaii.gov/ins/consumer/filing_a_complaint/

Idaho Department of Insurance 700 West State Street, 3rd Floor
P.O. Box 83720
Boise, ID 83720-0042 Ph: 208-334-4250
http://www.doi.idaho.gov/consumer/co mplaint.aspx

Illinois Department of Insurance 320 W. Washington St., 4th Floor
Springfield, IL 62767
217-782-4515. 866-445-5364
DOI.Director@illinois.gov http://www.insurance.illinois.gov

Illinois Department of Insurance
122 S. Michigan Ave., 19th Floor
Chicago, IL 60603 312-814-2420
https://mc.insurance.illinois.gov/messagecenter.nsf

Indiana Department of Insurance Attn: Consumer Services Division
311 W Washington Street, Suite 300
Indianapolis IN 46204-2787
800-622-4461 Fax: 317-234-2103
http://www.in.gov/idoi/2552.htm

Iowa Insurance Division
601 Locust St. - 4th Floor
Des Moines, IA 50309
515-281-5705. 877-955-1212
market.regulation@iid.iowa.gov
http://www.iid.state.ia.us/file_a_complaint

Kansas Insurance Department, Consumer Assistance Division Kansas
Department of Insurance
420 SW 9th Street
Topeka, KS 66612
800-432-2484 785-296-3071, 785-296-7829
commissioner@ksinsurance.org
http://www.ksinsurance.org/department/complaint.php

Kentucky Department of Insurance Consumer Protection Division
PO Box 517
Frankfort KY 40602-0517
800-595-6053 consumerservices@ky.gov http://insurance.ky.gov

Louisiana Department of Insurance PO Box 94214
Baton Rouge, LA 70804
800-259-5300, 800-259-5301 225-342-5900
https://www.ldi.la.gov/onlineservices/ConsumerComplaintForm

Maine Consumers for Affordable Health Care 12 Church Street, PO
Box 2490
Augusta, ME 04338-2490. 800-965-7476
Consumerhealth@mainecahc.org www.mainecahc.org

Maryland Office of the Attorney General Health Education and
Advocacy Unit 200 St. Paul Place, 16th Floor
Baltimore, MD 21202
877-261-8807
heau@oag.state.md.us
http://www.oag.state.md.us/Consumer.HEAU.htm

Massachusetts Health Care for All
One Federal Street
Boston, MA 02110 800-272-4232
www.massconsumerassistance.org

Michigan Health Insurance Consumer Assistance Program (HICAP)
Michigan Department of Insurance and Financial Services (DIFS)
PO Box 30220
Lansing, MI 48909-7720
877-999-6442
Difs-HICAP@michigan.gov http://www.michigan.gov.difs

Minnesota Department of Commerce 85 7th Place East, Suite 280
Saint Paul, MN 55101 651-539-1600
Consumer.protection@state.mn.us
https://mn.gov/commerce/consumers/file-a-complaint/

Health Help Mississippi
800 North President Street
Jackson, MS 39202 877-314-3843
healthhelpms@mhap.org http://healthhelpms.org

Missouri Department of Insurance
Harry S. Truman State Office Building Room 530 PO Box 690
Jefferson City, MO 65102 800-726-7390
consumeraffairs@insurance.mo.gov
www.insurance.mo.gov/consumers

Office of the Montana State Auditor Commissioner of Securities and
Insurance
840 Helena Avenue
Helena, MT 59601 800-332-6148
http://www.montanahealthanswers.com

Nebraska Department of Insurance Consumer Affairs
PO Box 82089
Lincoln, NE 68501
877-564-7323
402-471-0888
Fax: 402-471-4610
DOI.ConsumerAffairs@nebraska.gov
https://doi.nebraska.gov/consumer/consumer-assistance

Nevada Office of Consumer Health Assistance Governor's Consumer
Health Advocate
555 East Washington Avenue #4800
Las Vegas, NV 89101
702-486-3587. 888-333-1597 Cha@govcha.nv.gov http://dhhs.nv.gov

New Hampshire Department of Insurance
21 South Fruit Street, Suite 14
Concord, NH 03301 800-852-3416
consumerservices@ins.nh.gov http://www.nh.gov/insurance

New Jersey Department of Banking and Insurance 20 West State
Street, PO Box 325
Trenton, NJ 08625
800-446-7467, 609-292-7272 ombudsman@dobi.state.nj.us
http://www.state.nj.us.dobi/consumer.htm

New Mexico Public Regulation Commission Consumer Relations
Division
1120 Paseo De Peralta Santa Fe, NM 87504
855-857-0972, 888-427-5772
Fax: 505-476-0326 Mchb.grievance@state.nm.us
http://nmprc.state.nm.us/consumer-relations/index.html

Community Service Society of New York Community Health
Advocates
633 Third Avenue, 10th Floor
New York, NY 10017 888-614-5400 cha@cssny.org
http://www.communityhealthadvocates.org/ 800-400-8882
https://www.health.ny.gov/health_care/managed_care/appealext.htm
http://www.dfs.ny.gov/insurance/extapp/extappqa.htm

North Carolina Department of Insurance Health Insurance Smart NC
430 N. Salisbury Street Suite 1018
Raleigh, NC 27603
855-408-1212
https://www.ncdoi.gov/consumers/health-insurance

North Dakota State Insurance Department
600 East Boulevard Avenue
Bismarck, ND 58505-0320
800-247-0560 insurance@nd.gov
https://www.insurance.nd.gov/consumers/complaints

Ohio Department of Insurance
50 W. Town Street, Suite 300
Columbus, Ohio 43215
614-644-2658 800-686-1526
https://insurance.ohio.gov/wps/portal/gov/odi/about-
us/complaintcenter/complaint-center-1

Oklahoma Insurance Department Five Corporate Plaza
3625 Northwest 56th Street, Suite100
Oklahoma City, OK 73112-4511
800-522-0071, 405-521-2828
https://www.ok.gov/oid/Consumers/Consumer_Assistance/

Oregon Health Connect
1435 NE 81st Avenue, Suite 500
Portland, OR 97213-6759
866-698-6155
healthconnect@211info.org http://211info.org/health/

Pennsylvania Insurance Department
1326 Strawberry Square
Harrisburg, PA 17120
877-881-6388 http://www.insurance.pa.gov

Rhode Island Consumer Assistance Program
1210 Pontiac Avenue
Cranston, RI 02920 855-747-3224
rireach@ripin.org http://www.rireach.org/

South Carolina Department of Insurance Consumer and Individual
Licensing Services
PO Box 100105
Columbia, SC 29202
803-737-6180
consumers@doi.sc.gov http://www.doi.sc.gov/638/Health-Insurance

South Dakota Department of Labor and Regulation
124 South Euclid Avenue, 2nd floor
Pierre, SD 57501 605-773-3563
sdinsurance@state.sd.us
https://dlr.sd.gov/insurance/doi_complaint.aspx

Tennessee Department of Commerce & Insurance
500 James Robertson Parkway
Davy Crockett Tower, 4th floor
Nashville, TN 37243-0565
615-741-2241
http://www.tn.gov/commerce/section/consumer-services

Texas Consumer Health Assistance Program Texas Department of
Insurance
Mail Code 111-1A
333 Guadalupe, PO Box 149091
Austin, TX 78714-9091
800-252-3439
ConsumerProtection@tdi.texas.gov http://www.texashealthoptions.com

Utah Insurance Department
350 N. State Street
State Office Building Room 3110
Salt Lake City, UT 84114
801-538-3800 Salt Lake City area 800-439-3805 Toll free In-State
https://insurance.utah.gov/complaint

Vermont Legal Aid
264 North Winooski Avenue
Burlington, VT 05402
800-889-2047 www.vtlegalaid.org

Virginia State Corporation Commission
Life & Health Division, Bureau of Insurance
PO Box 1157
Richmond, VA 23218 804-371-9691
bureauofinsurance@scc.virginia.gov
http://www.scc.virginia.gov/boi/cons/index.aspx

Washington Consumer Assistance Program
5000 Capitol Blvd.
Tumwater, WA 98501
800-562-6900 cap@oic.wa.gov https://www.insurance.wa.gov/

West Virginia Offices of the Insurance Commissioner Consumer
Service Division
PO Box 50540
Charleston, WV 25305-0540
888-879-9842
http://www.wvinsurance.gov/ConsumerServices/ConsumerServices.asp
x

Wisconsin Office of the Commissioner of Insurance
PO Box 7873
Madison, WI 53707-7873
800-236-8517 608-266-0103
ocicomplaints@wisconsin.gov
https://oci.wi.gov/Pages/Consumers/GrievancesComplaints.aspx

Wyoming Insurance Department
106 E. 6th Avenue
Cheyenne, WY 82001
307-777-7402 800-438-5768
http://doi.wyo.gov/consumers/consumer-request-for-assistance/file-
acomplaint

Putting it all into Action

Now that you've gained insights into what it takes to maximize your health insurance, it's time to put it all into action. Health insurance literacy skills can be learned and developed with practice. Here's a checklist of exercises you can do to build confidence and be ready to keep more money in your pocket.

- Register / log into your health insurance plan website
- Print or Order an ID card
- Review what's covered by your plan
- Locate the explanation of benefits (EOB) section on the plan's website
- Search for a doctor or health provider in your zip code
- Setup your preferences, notification settings and contact information (do you want to receive paper statements or electronic only when claims are processed?)
- Find the cost of care tool; practice searching for the cost of procedures (look up prior services like an office visit, radiology or physical therapy)
- Locate how to file a claim (submit online, download PDF claim form)
- Identify how to contact customer service by phone, email, chat
- Review your paystub or premium statements at least quarterly each year to confirm you are paying correct amount for your health insurance
- Review and make benefit changes (annually) during open enrollment period; don't miss the submission deadlines
- Proactively read or look for benefit communications and plan materials from your employer or health insurance plan via e-mail or mail (information is often posted to a website or employer intranet)
- Submit new hire or mid-year life event changes timely (typically within 30 days of becoming eligible for new coverage or losing other coverage)
- File your health claims for reimbursement timely with your health

insurance plan (out-of-network claims are your responsibility to file).

- Confirm filing deadlines which may be posted on a claim form. 90 or 180 days is common.

  FSA claims will have a different deadline, typically 2 ½ months after the prior calendar year ends, but could be different so check with your plan

- If your child is enrolled, confirm how long they can remain on the plan. Age 26 is a common limit. Confirm if through the date of birth or the end of the month the child turns age 26. Children who age-out of a plan are eligible to continue with the same plan through COBRA

- Schedule annual checkups and periodic routine visits. Verify how often you can go to get routine visits (every 12 months rolling period or every calendar year)

These action items are not exhaustive and can change due to new insurance regulations or plan design updates made by your health plan. Keep current in any number of ways:

- Look for communications from your health insurance plan
- Follow your health insurance company on LinkedIn or Facebook, or read their public internet page
- Read communications distributed by your employer
- Keep a notebook or folder of your plan information and review annually

Additional HIL Best Practices

- o Document your health insurance activity: Maintain a folder, a journal or notebook
- o Don't pay up front for healthcare services; wait until health insurance processes your claim
- o Review your EOBs first to identify what you owe *before* paying for a service: *Compare amount due to invoices sent from the provider*
- o Ask healthcare providers up front what services may be performed and whether covered by the plan
- o Get access to your health insurance materials & resources (SBC, Benefit Summary). *Print new copies every year*
- o Register with / use the health plan website or mobile app

Health Insurance Terms

Deductible - The amount you owe for covered health care services before your health insurance or plan begins to pay. Your first dollar obligation.

Coinsurance % - Your share of the cost for a covered health care service, usually calculated as a percentage (like 20%) of the allowed amount for the service.

Copay - An amount you pay as your share of the cost for a medical service or item, like a doctor's visit. A flat amount like $20.

Maximum-out-of-pocket - The most you have to pay for covered services in a plan year. After you spend this amount on deductibles, copayments, and coinsurance for in-network care and services, your health plan pays 100% of the costs of covered benefits. Excludes: premiums / payroll contributions, costs above allowed amount for a service, services not covered.

Network Provider - The doctors, hospitals, and suppliers your health insurer has contracted with to deliver health care services to their enrolled members. Agreed to accept negotiated rates (which may be lower than normal charges).

Allowed Amount or Negotiated Discount - The maximum amount a plan will pay for a covered health care service. May also be called "eligible expense", "payment allowance", or "negotiated rate."

Health Insurance Premium - The amount you pay for your health insurance or plan each month. Could be considered payroll contribution through employer.

Drug Formulary - A list of prescription drugs covered by a prescription drug plan or another insurance plan offering prescription drug benefits.

Explanation of Benefits (EOB) - An EOB is a statement describing what costs the health plan covered for medical care or services you received. The EOB is generated when your provider submits a claim for the services you received. Identifies any out-of-pocket medical expenses you are responsible for.

High Deductible Health Plan (HDHP) - A plan with a higher deductible than a traditional insurance plan. The monthly premium is usually lower, but you pay more health care costs yourself before the insurance company starts to pay its share (your deductible). A high deductible plan (HDHP) can be combined with a health savings account (HSA), allowing you to pay for certain medical expenses with money free from federal taxes.

For 2023, the IRS defines a high deductible health plan as any plan with a deductible of at least $1,400 for an individual or $2,800 for a family. These amounts will increase to $1,500 and $3,000 respectively in 2024.

Health Insurance Literacy Quiz

1. **Which of the following is the best definition of the term "health insurance premium?"**
   A. The best type of health insurance you can buy
   B. The amount health insurance companies charge each month for coverage
   C. A bonus you get at the end of the year if you stay covered
   D. The amount you owe after health insurance processes your claim

2. **Which of the following is the best definition of the term "annual health insurance deductible?"**
   A. The amount that is deducted from your paycheck each year to pay for your policy
   B. The amount of health expenses you can subtract from income on your yearly tax return
   C. The amount of covered health care expenses you must pay yourself each year before your insurance will pay

3. **Which of the following best describes the "annual out-of-pocket limit" under a health insurance policy?**
   A. The most you will have to pay in deductibles, copays, and coinsurance
   B. for covered care received in network for the year
   C. The most your insurance policy will pay for covered services in a year
   D. The most you will have to pay premiums in a year

4. **Suppose that under your health insurance policy, hospital expenses are subject to a $1,000 deductible and a $250 per day copay. You get sick and are hospitalized for 4 days, and the bill (after insurance discounts are applied) comes to $6,000. How much of the hospital bill will you have to pay yourself?**
   A. $0.00
   B. $1,000
   C. $2,000
   D. $4,000

5. **Which of the following best describes a "health insurance formulary?**
    A. The form you send to your insurance company when you need to have a medical bill paid
    B. The permission type you must get from your insurance company before surgery will be covered
    C. The list of prescription drugs your health plan will cover

6. **Which of the following best describes a health plan "provider network?"**
    A. The computer system doctors and hospitals use to submit bills to
    B. insurance companies
    C. The hospitals and doctors that contract with your health plan to provide services for an agreed-upon rate or fee schedule
    D. A website where consumers can find information about the best doctors

7. **What is a Summary of Benefits and Coverage?**
    A. The claims statement a health insurance creates after a claim is paid
    B. An easy-to-read summary that lets you make apples-to-apples
    C. comparisons of costs and coverage between health plans
    D. Summary of your HIPAA Rights provided by your doctor at the time
    E. of a visit

8. **True or false: If you receive inpatient care at a hospital that participates
    in your health plan's provider network, all the doctors who care for
    you while you're in the hospital will also be in-network.**
    A. True
    B. False

9. Suppose your health plan covers lab tests in full if you go to an in-network lab, but only pays 60% of allowed charges if you go out-of-network. You forget to check and go get your blood test at a lab that turns out to be out-of-network. The lab bills you $100 for the blood test. Your health insurance allows only a $20 charge for that test. How much would you have to pay out-of-pocket for that lab test?
   A. $0.00
   B. $40.00
   C. $80.00
   D. $88.00

10. True or false? If your health insurance or health plan refuses to pay for a service that you think is covered and your doctor says you need, you can appeal the denial and possibly get the insurance company to pay the claim.
    A. True
    B. False

Questions from this quiz are based upon the Kaiser Family Foundation (KFF) Health Insurance Quiz available on https://www.kff.org/quiz/health-insurance-quiz/

Quiz Answers

1. B
2. C
3. A
4. C $1,000 deductible plus ($250 / day x 4 days) = $2,000
5. C
6. B
7. B
8. B
9. D $100 minus ($20 x .60) = $88
10. A

Disclaimer

The information provided in this book is for informational purposes only and is not intended to be a source of advice, nor does the information and/or documents contained in this book constitute legal or financial advice and should never be used without first consulting with your health insurance plan, benefits specialist or other professional advisor including plan specific documents and materials to identify the relevant details of your health insurance plan to determine what may be best for your individual needs.

The publisher and the author do not make any guarantee or other promise as to any results that may be obtained from using the content of this book. To the maximum extent permitted by law, the publisher and the author disclaim any and all liability in the event any information, commentary, analysis, opinions, advice and/or recommendations contained in this book prove to be inaccurate, incomplete or unreliable, or result in any investment or other losses

Notes

Notes for "Introduction"

1.   "Findings from the 2023 Consumer Engagement in Health Care Survey", Employee Benefit Research Institute March 19, 2024; https://www.ebri.org/docs/default-source/webinars/cehcs_031924.pdf?sfvrsn=ce5f072f_3

2.   "2019 Aflac WorkForces Report, 12 Trends Influencing the Future of Workplace Benefits", accessed November 24, 2019; https://www.aflac.com/business/resources/aflac-workforcesreport/default.aspx

3.   "Health Insurance Coverage in the United States: 2023", Census.gov, Issued September 2024, accessed February 15, 2025;https://www.census.gov/library/publications/2024/demo/p60-284.html

4."2024 Employer Health Benefits Survey", Henry J. Kaiser Family Foundation, accessed February 15, 2025, https://files.kff.org/attachment/Employer-Health-Benefits-Survey-2024-Annual-Survey.pdf

5.   "Cost-Sharing for Plans Offered in the Federal Marketplace 2023," The Henry J. Kaiser Family Foundation, accessed February 15, 2025; https://files.kff.org/attachment/Cost-Sharing-for-Plans-Offered-in-the-Federal-Marketplace-2023.pptx

6.   "The Average Savings Account Balance, Updated February 11, 2025; accessed February 15, 2025; https://www.fool.com/money/research/average-savings-account-balance/

7. Bankruptcy Statistics:
   https://www.debt.org/bankruptcy/statistics/
   https://www.debt.org/bankruptcy/medical/

8. "The Burden of Medical Debt: Results from The Kaiser
   Family Foundation/New York Time Medical Bills Survey,"
   The Henry J.
   Kaiser Family Foundation, January 5, 2016, accessed March 25,
   2017, http://kff.org/health-costs/report/the-burden-of-medical-
   debtresults-from- the-kaiser-family-foundationnew-york-times-
   medicalbills-survey/

9. ValuePenguin analysis of State Health Compare tool data
   https://www.valuepenguin.com/high-deductible-health-plan-study

10. A Survey of Americans with High-Deductible Health Plans
    Identifies Opportunities to Enhance Consumer Behaviors, Health
    Affairs March 2019.

11. Significant Disparities Exist in Consumer Health
    Insurance Literacy: Implications for Health Care Reform.
    HLRP: Health Literacy Research and Practice, Vol. 3,
    No. 4, 2019. Jean Edward, PhD, RN; Amanda Wiggins,
    PhD; Malea Hoepf Young, MPH, CHES; and Mary Kay
    Rayens PhD.

12. Results from Kaiser Family Foundation Health Insurance
    Quiz, question #9. https://www.kff.org/quiz/health-
    insurance-quiz/

13. New Data Reveals Consumers Still Struggle with Health care Literacy. Managed Healthcare Executive, July 26, 2022. https://www.managedhealthcareexecutive.com/view/new - datareveals-consumers-still-struggle-with-healthcare-literacy

14. Americans Confused by Basic Health Insurance Terms But Happy With Their Plans. Les Masterson. Updated July 18, 2022. Forbes Advisor online: https://www.forbes.com/advisor/healthinsurance/confused-by-health- insurance-terms/

15. Opportunities to Enhance the Utility of Electronic Health Care Claims. CAQH Core, April 2023; accessed February 15, 2025. https://www.caqh.org/hubfs/43908627/drupal/2023-05/CORE%20-%20HC%20Claims%20Issue%20Brief%20Final.pdf

Notes for "Be an Active Consumer of Your Health Insurance"

1. American Medical Association, accessed March 25, 2017, https://www.ama-assn.org/practice-management/cpt?-pprocesshow- code-becomes-code=

2. "The Burden of Medical Debt: Results from The Kaiser Family Foundation/New York Time Medical Bills Survey," The Henry J.
Kaiser Family Foundation, January 5, 2016, accessed March 25, 2017, kff.org/health-costs/report/the-burden-of-medical-debtresults-from-the- kaiser-foundationnew-york-times-medical-billssurvey/.

3. "2024 U.S. Generic & Biosimilar Medicines Savings Report" Association for Accessible Medicines, accessed February 15, 2025, https://accessiblemeds.org/resources/blog/2024-savings-report/

4. "2024 U.S. Generic & Biosimilar Medicines Savings Report" Association for Accessible Medicines, accessed February 15, 2025, https://accessiblemeds.org/resources/blog/2024-savings-report/ (power point slides)

5. "Paying Physicians to Prescribe Generic Drugs and Follow-On Biologics in the United States," Nation Center for Biotechnology Information, U.S. National Library of Medicine, PLoS Med. 2015 Mar; 12(3):e1001802, https://www.ncbi.nlm.nih.gov/pmc/articles/PMC4363899/.

6. "Impact of Alternative Interventions on Changes in Generic Dispensing Rates," National Center for Biotechnology Information, Health Serv Res. 2006 Oct; 41(5): 1876-1894.

7. "Don't get hooked on prescription-drug coupons." Consumer Reports, March 2012, accessed March 25, 2017, http://www.consumerreports.org/cro/2012/03/don-t-get-hooked- onprescription-drug-coupons/index.htm

8. "Using a Mail Order Pharmacy Doesn't Always Save You Money," Consumer Reports, March 2016, accessed March 25, 2017, http://www.consumerreports.org/pharmacies/mail-orderpharmacy-doesnt-always-save-money/

9. "The Burden of Medical Debt: Results from The Kaiser Family Foundation/New York Time Medical Bills Survey," The Henry J. Kaiser Family Foundation, January 5, 2016, accessed March 25,
2017, kff.org/health-costs/report/the-burden-of-medical-debtresults- from-the-kaiser-foundationnew-york-times-medical-billssurvey/.

Notes for "Keep More Money in Your Pocket"

1. Publication 969 (2024), Health Savings Accounts and Other Tax-Favored Health Plans. Accessed February 15, 2025. https://www.irs.gov/publications/p969#:~:text=If%20you%20have%20family%20HDHP,can%20contribute%20up%20to%20%248%2C300.&text=For%202025%2C%20if%20you%20have,can%20contribute%20up%20to%20%248%2C550.

2. IRS: Healthcare FSA reminder: Employees can contribute up to $3,300 in 2025; must elect every year. November 7, 2024. Accessed February 15, 2025. https://www.irs.gov/newsroom/irs-healthcare-fsa-reminder-employees-can-contribute-up-to-3300-in-2025-must-elect-every-year#:~:text=For%20FSAs%20that%20permit%20the,%24640%20in%20tax%20year%202024

3. 2022 Employer Health Benefits Survey, Henry J. Kaiser Family Foundation, accessed February 15, 2025, https://www.kff.org/report-section/ehbs-2022-section-13-employer-practices-telehealth-provider-networks-and-coverage-for-mental-health-services/#:~:text=The%20percentages%20of%20small%20firms,firms)%20%5BFigure%2013.3%5D.

4.   "Telehealth and Virtual Care Policy Position Statement", Business Group on Health, January 1, 2024; accessed February 15, 2025. https://www.businessgrouphealth.org/Resources/Business-Group-on-Healths-Position-Statement-on-Telehealth

5.   MDLIVE Telehealth Utilization Whitepaper: https://www.mdlive.com/wp-content/uploads/2018/03/MDLIVE_TelehealthUtilization_Whitepaper.pdf

6.   Telehealth Market Outlook 2028, Transparency Market Research. Accessed February 15, 2025. https://www.transparencymarketresearch.com/telehealth-market.html

Notes for "Appealing Your Claim"

1. Claims Denials and Appeals in ACA Marketplace Plans in 2023. Kaiser Family Foundation, January 27, 2025. Accessed February 15, 2025. **https://www.kff.org/private-insurance/issue-brief/claims-denials-and-appeals-in-aca-marketplace-plans-in-2023/**

www.ingramcontent.com/pod-product-compliance
Lightning Source LLC
Chambersburg PA
CBHW071851200326
41519CB00016B/4338